Domino

Student's Book 4

Angela Llanas • Libby Williams

MACMILLAN
HEINEMANN
English Language Teaching

Contents

UNIT 1 Karate kids — page 4

Key structures
Review
Are there any nuts?
Is there any chocolate sauce?
The children left the ice-cream parlor.
How old are you?
They got up at six.
He didn't do his homework.

Vocabulary
Ice-cream parlor
Karate class

Make It
Karate headband
Story Book
How old are you?
Fact File
Baseball

UNIT 2 Work and play — page 14

Key structures
He always/sometimes/never gets up early.
I sometimes/never/always eat fish.
She wants to be a pilot.
How often do you visit your dentist? Once, twice, three times …
It's a quarter to three.
It's a quarter after five.

Vocabulary
Professions
Words of frequency

Make It
Homework pouch
Story Book
Detective Tiger
Fact File
Firefighters

UNIT 3 In the country — page 24

Key structures
My backpack isn't as heavy as yours.
Horseback riding is more exciting than swimming.
It's smaller, but it's more comfortable.
He took the children rafting.
The river went faster.
There aren't as many apples as before.

Vocabulary
Camping
Outdoor activities
Adjectives

Make It
Campfire picture
Story Book
The black pony
Fact File
Ponies

UNIT 4 The International Center — page 34

Key structures
I'm from Mexico.
I'm Mexican.
I speak Spanish.
They went into the pyramid.
What time is it?
What does he look like?

Vocabulary
Countries
Nationalities
Languages

Make It
Spanish fan
Story Book
The escalator
Fact File
Ancient Egypt

UNIT 5 Creepy crawlies — page 44

Key structures
She's good at art.
He's bad at writing stories.
I'm scared of snakes.
I'm not interested in feeding it.
It was too small.
He isn't tall enough.
It's a beautiful, green snake.

Vocabulary
School subjects
Emotions and interests

Make It
Snake draft stopper
Story Book
Herbert's white rat
Fact File
Spiders

UNIT 6 Noises in the night — page 54

Key structures
She was running.
They were eating.
He wasn't fighting.
What was he doing?
What were they doing?
Were you feeling sick?

Vocabulary
Actions and possibilities
Night workers

Make It
Comb tooters and drums
Story Book
Crash in the night
Fact File
Sound

UNIT 7 Lunar landscape — page 64

Key structures
It's the newest.
It's the nearest.
It's the most magnificent telescope I ever saw!
Who has the biggest balloon/the most comfortable chair?

Vocabulary
Planets and meteors

Make It
Lunar landscape
Story Book
Surprise on Pluto
Fact File
The Moon

UNIT 8 How do you get there? — page 74

Key structures
Go down the street.
Turn left/right.
How do you get to the nearest gas station?
Turn left at the video store.
Go past the drugstore.
Give it to me.
It went to …

Vocabulary
Directions
Locations

Make It
Needle compass
Story Book
The tennis trophy
Fact File
Water polo

UNIT 9 The girl from Number 5 — page 84

Key structures
She was wearing a skirt.
She was playing basketball.
The bus leaves at nine o'clock.
How long do we stay?
How long does it take?
The children were waiting.
The bus arrived.

Vocabulary
Timetables
Schedules

Make It
Stained-glass window
Story Book
Fast train, slow train
Fact File
Flying

UNIT 10 Black and white — page 94

Key structures
Everyone is hot. No one has any money.
No one is interested in anything.
Everyone is going to come.
How about asking your mother?

Vocabulary
Generalizations
Parties

Make It
Black-and-white party twisters
Story Book
Ronnie's invention
Fact File
Dominoes

games — page 104

Are there any nuts? Is there any chocolate sauce?

UNIT 1 Karate kids

Lesson 1

adj vanilla n chocolate chips ice-cream parlor sauce

1. Listen and act out.

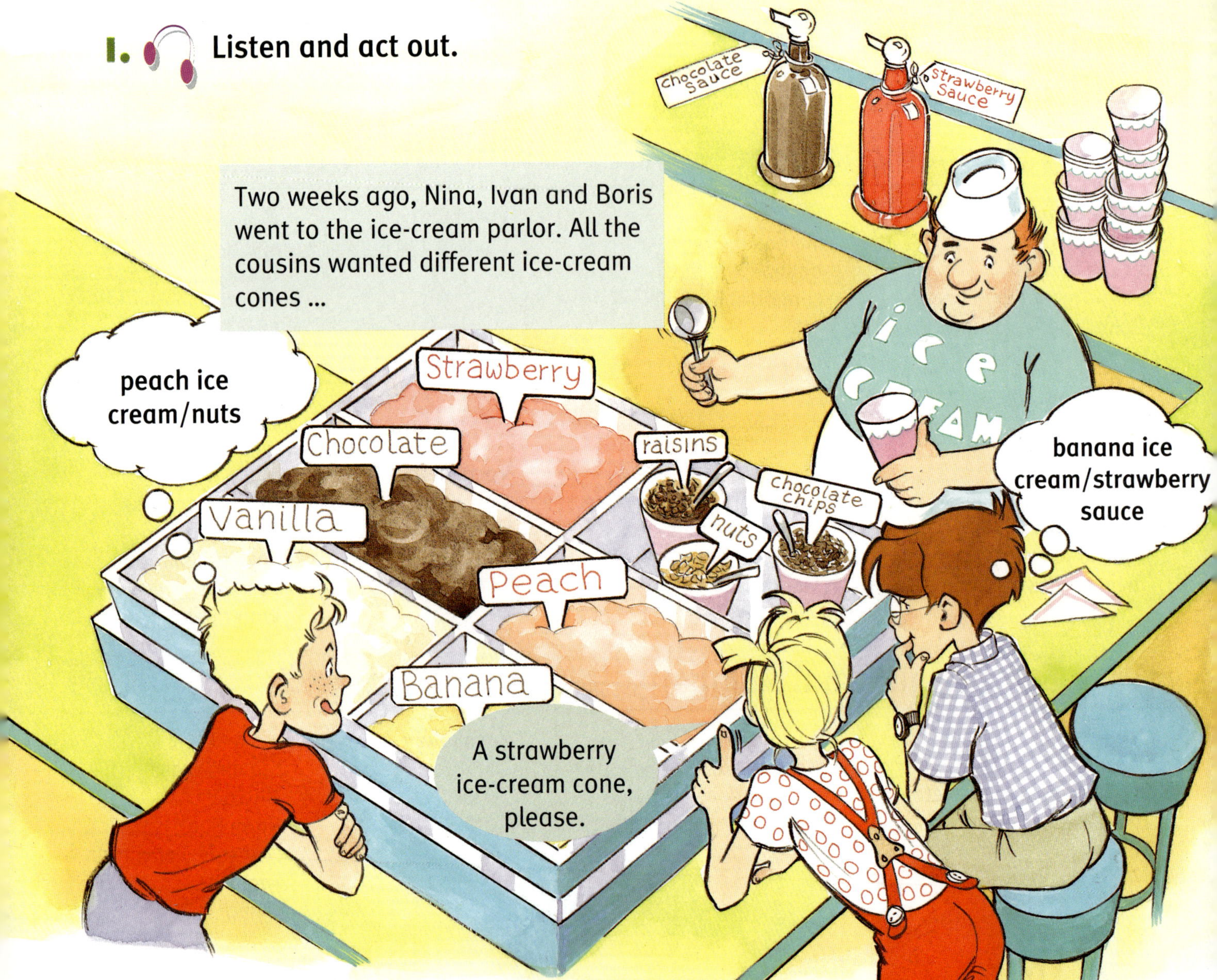

Two weeks ago, Nina, Ivan and Boris went to the ice-cream parlor. All the cousins wanted different ice-cream cones ...
chocolate sauce
strawberry sauce
peach ice cream/nuts
Strawberry
Chocolate
raisins
chocolate chips
nuts
Vanilla
Peach
Banana
banana ice cream/strawberry sauce
A strawberry ice-cream cone, please.

2. Act out Ivan and Boris's orders.

3. Work in pairs. Buy an ice-cream cone for you.

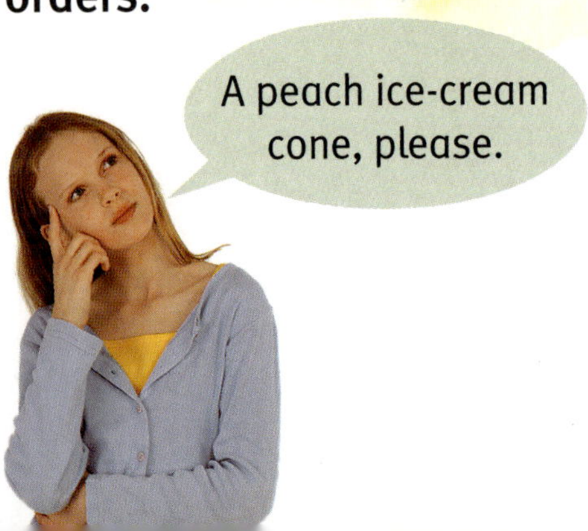

A peach ice-cream cone, please.

The children left the ice-cream parlor.

Lesson 2

1. Read and circle.

The children left the ice-cream parlor. They saw Nanook in the street. "Where are you going, Nanook?" shouted Ivan. "I'm going to my karate class," said Nanook. "Come with me." So the cousins went with Nanook to his karate class. Boris didn't like the class. But Ivan and Nina loved the class. They wanted to learn karate too.

a. The children saw Nanook in the ice-cream parlor.   yes   no
b. Nanook invited them to go with him.   yes   no
c. Boris loved the karate class.   yes   no
d. The twins liked the class.   yes   no

2. Talk about the karate class.

a. How many girls were there in the class?
b. How many boys were there?
c. What time was it?
d. Where did Ivan and Nina sit?
e. What did Boris do?

3. Practice. Complete the form. Tell the class.

Class
_____
Day
_____
Time
_____
Do you like it? _____

What extra class do you go to?

I go to Olympic gymnastics.

How old are you?

Lesson 3

n reception   uniform
adj advanced   beginners   intermediate

1. Read and answer.

KARATE CLASSES
Every Saturday morning.

Advanced   9 o'clock
Beginners   10 o'clock
Intermediate   11 o'clock

Buy your uniform in reception.

a. Is there a karate class for beginners?
b. What day is the class?
c. What time is it?
d. What do you need for the class?

2. Listen and complete.

Class <u>Karate for beginners</u>
Name(s) _____
Age(s) _____
Address _____
Phone number _____
Starting day _____

3. In pairs, choose your class. Fill in the form and act out.

ballet   ice skating   piano
computer skills   photography

Class _____
Name(s) _____
Age(s) _____
Address _____
Phone number _____
Starting day _____

Lesson 4

1. Make a karate headband.

YOU NEED
black paper   white paper
pencil   scissors   glue   stapler

UNIT 7
Make It

1. Cut out a long strip of black paper to go around your head.

2. Draw a symbol on a small piece of white paper.

3. Cut it out and glue it on the black band.

4. Measure the band around your head and staple it.

2. Sing along.

I don't like skating,
I don't like skiing,
I don't like swimming
   and I never did.
I only like karate,
'Cos I'm the Karate Kid.

I don't watch
   basketball,
I don't watch volleyball,
I don't watch soccer
   and I never did.
I only watch karate,
'Cos I'm the Karate Kid!

Lesson 5 — Check what you know

1. Read and order.

a. _____
b. _____
c. _____
d. _____
e. _____
f. _____
g. _____

When are they?
Yes, there are.
Are there any computer classes for beginners?
Great! What's your name?
On Wednesday afternoons at five thirty.
Wednesdays? Good! I'd like to come.
Kelly Lynch.

2. Complete the story. Use these verbs.

| talk | buy | ~~go~~ | look at | leave | play |

Kelly _went_ with her father to the computer store. They _____ lots of computers. Kelly's father _____ to the man in the store. Kelly _____ computer games. Then they _____ the store. Kelly's father didn't buy a computer, but he _____ two big ice-cream cones!

Spelling corner

a. 🍓 s_____
b. 🍊 p_____
c. (beans) r_____
d. 🍦 v_____
   i_____ _____
e. 🍒  c_____

They got up at six.

UNIT 1

Lesson 6

n exercises   piece of wood
v break   hit   laugh   learn

1. Read and write the past tense of each verb.

a. get   _got_____   d. break _____   g. drive _____
b. watch _____   e. have   _____   h. talk   _____
c. put   _____   f. hit   _____   i. learn _____

Last Saturday, the twins got up at six o'clock. They were very excited. They put on their new karate uniforms and they had breakfast.

Their mother drove them to the class. The twins talked about karate all the way.

First, they watched the advanced students. One of the students broke a piece of wood. It hit Ivan's leg, but it didn't hurt him. Nina laughed a lot.

Then they had their class. They learned lots of exercises. It was fun.

2. Act out in groups of three.

3. Sing along. Write two more verses.

Last Saturday, I played **soccer**,
And that was really fun,
And then I bought **some ice cream**,
And ate it in the sun.

What did you do today?

We ...

Did you have a good time?

9

Lesson 7

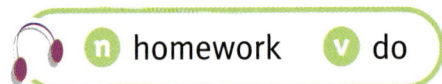

He didn't do his homework.

1. Read the story.

It was Saturday. Millie and Martin did their  in the morning.

Then they had  in Martin's house with Katy.

In the afternoon, they went to their  class. In the evening they

watched  at Millie's house with Benjamin. It was "Karate Kid 5."

2. Now talk about Boris's day.

Boris didn't do his homework on Saturday morning. He went ...

3. Write and say.

Plan a fun day for next Saturday.
Where? _____
Who with? _____
When? _____
Activities? _____

Next Saturday, I'm going to ...

Lesson 8 — How old are you?

1.  **Listen and read.**

1
Kurt looked at the board in the Junior Club. "How about karate?" asked his mom.
"No, the weight-lifting class, please!" said Kurt.

2
"How old are you?" asked the receptionist. "The children in the weight-lifting class are fifteen or older.
"I'm fifteen," said Kurt. But he was twelve.

3
At his first class, Kurt watched the instructor. "Can I do that?" he asked.
"How old are you?" asked the instructor.
"Fifteen," said Kurt.

4
But the weight was very heavy! Kurt hurt a muscle.
"*How* old are you?" asked the instructor.
"Twelve," said Kurt.
"So don't say you're fifteen. Weights are dangerous for children."

2. Write the answers.

a. Which class did Kurt go to?
b. How old is he?
c. How old were the other children in the class?
d. What did he hurt? Why?

Lesson 9

Fact File — Baseball

1. Read and label.

Baseball is a very popular sport in the United States and Canada. Some countries in Latin America also play it. In a baseball game, there are two teams. Each team has nine players. Mark the position of the missing players on the baseball ground.

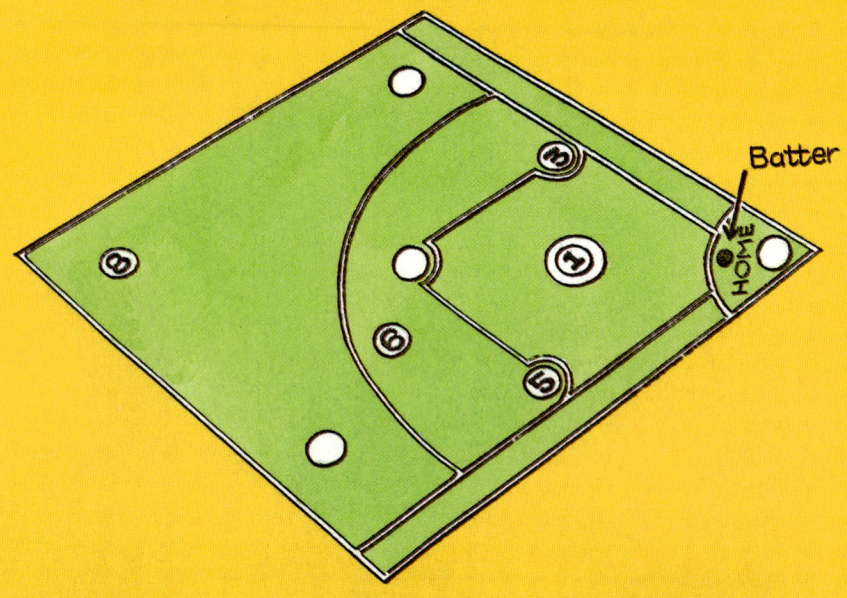

1. Pitcher
2. Catcher
3. First base
4. Second base
5. Third base
6. Short stop
7. Left fielder
8. Center fielder
9. Right fielder

Baseball players wear special clothes. Label the picture.

cap
shirt
undershirt
short pants
long socks
shoes with spikes

This is their special equipment.

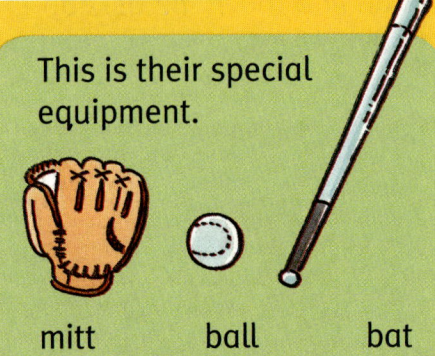

mitt   ball   bat

2. Describe another team game.

a. Where do people play it?
b. What do they wear?
c. What special equipment do they use?

12

Lesson 10 — Show what you know

1. Complete the story.

like   go   not be   put   break
watch   skate   laugh

Danny and Cathy _____ to their first skating class last Friday. First, they _____ on their skates. Then they _____ the teacher. Then *they* tried. It _____ easy! Danny fell over! He _____ his pencil, but he didn't hurt himself! Cathy _____ a lot. They both _____ the class. " We love _____ ," they said.

2. Write questions about the story.

a. _____ ? Last Friday.
b. _____ first? They put on their skates.
c. _____? His pencil.
d. _____? Yes, they did.

3. Answer the questions about you.

a. How old are you?
b. What's your phone number?
c. What did you do yesterday afternoon?
d. What do you like doing?
e. What extra classes do you take and when do you take them?
f. Write five things you have in your schoolbag or lunch bag now.

You're a winner!

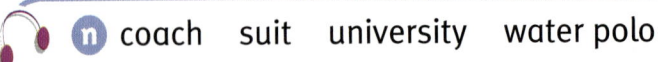
He always/sometimes/never gets up early.

UNIT 2 Work and play

n coach   suit   university   water polo

Lesson 1

1. Listen, read and find out.

   a. Who is he?
   b. Where does he work?
   c. What does he do?
   d. Does he get up early every day?
   e. Does he go swimming every evening?

   Alex Boski is the twins' father. He works at Redwood University. He's the new water-polo coach. He always gets up at six o'clock and he always runs in the park before breakfast. He sometimes goes swimming in the evening. He never wears a suit to work. Alex Boski loves his job.

2. Talk about the children.

	always	sometimes	never
get up early		👦👦	👦
run in the park		👦👦	👦
wear uniform to school			👦👦👦
eat at home	👦	👦👦	
do homework (afternoon)	👦		👦👦
watch TV (evening)	👦👦	👦	
do experiments		👦	👦👦

Boris never gets up early

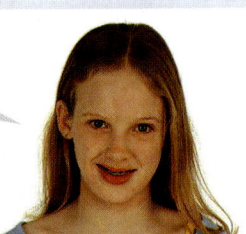

I sometimes/never/always eat fish.

UNIT 2

Lesson 2

cereal   diet   pasta   salad

1. Listen and draw lines. Talk about Randy's diet.

Wow! What do you have for breakfast, Randy?

Randy's Diet

Breakfast — always / sometimes

Lunch — always / sometimes

Supper — always / sometimes

never

He always has fruit for breakfast.

2. Practice.

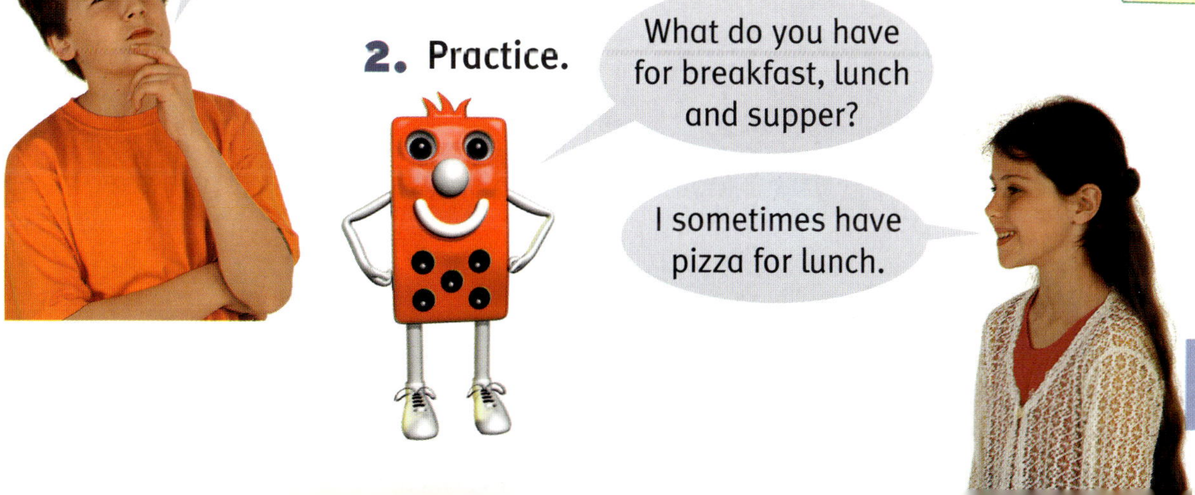

What do you have for breakfast, lunch and supper?

I sometimes have pizza for lunch.

Lesson 3

n chef   pilot   scientist   soccer player   vet   v grow up

She wants to be a pilot.

1. Listen and answer.

What do you want to be when you grow up?

a. What's Miss Mitzi's profession?
b. Why did she choose it?
c. What does Martin want to be?
d. Why?
e. What does Millie want to be?
f. Why?

2. Continue.

Ivan, what do you want to be when you grow up?

3. Practice. Talk about you.

What do you want to be?

I want to be ...

16

Lesson 4

YOU NEED
paper   stapler   crayons   felt-tip pen

UNIT 2 — Make It

1. Make a professions pouch for your homework.

1 Fold the paper.

2 Staple along the sides.

3 Decorate your pouch with professions – words and pictures.

2. 🎧 Sing along.

When I grow up,
I don't want to be
A doctor or a dentist,
That's not for me.

When I grow up,
I'd like to be
An astronaut –
That's right for me!

Lesson 5 — Check what you know

1. Write the sentences with *always*, *never* or *sometimes*.

	Monday	Tuesday	Wednesday	Thursday	Friday
get up late	✓	✓		✓	
have bread for breakfast	✓	✓	✓	✓	✓
arrive at school late					
read in bed		✓		✓	✓

a. get up late _____ He sometimes gets up late. _____

b. have bread for breakfast _____

c. arrive at school late _____

d. read in bed _____

2. Follow the lines. Write sentences.

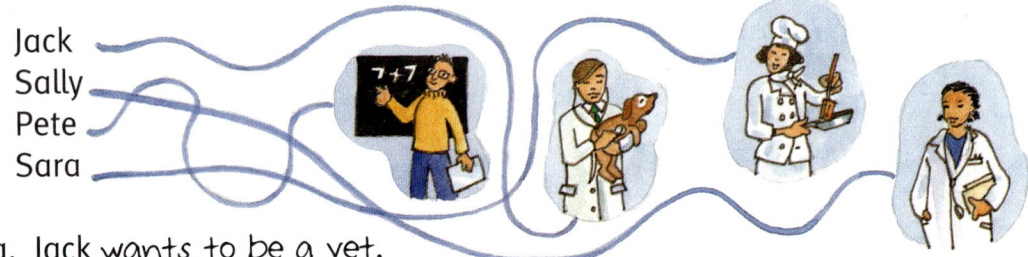

a. Jack wants to be a vet. _____

b. Sally _____

c. Pete _____

d. Sara _____

Spelling corner

a.  s_____

b.  s_____ p_____

c.  f_____

d.  a_____

e. s_____

How often do you visit your dentist? Once, twice, three times ...

UNIT 2

Lesson 6

adv once   twice   three times   v change

1. Listen and match. What is Dr. Jackson's advice?

a. Visit your dentist   1. three times a day.
b. Brush your teeth   2. twice a year.
c. Use dental floss   3. once a month.
d. Change your toothbrush 4. once a week.

How often do you visit your dentist?

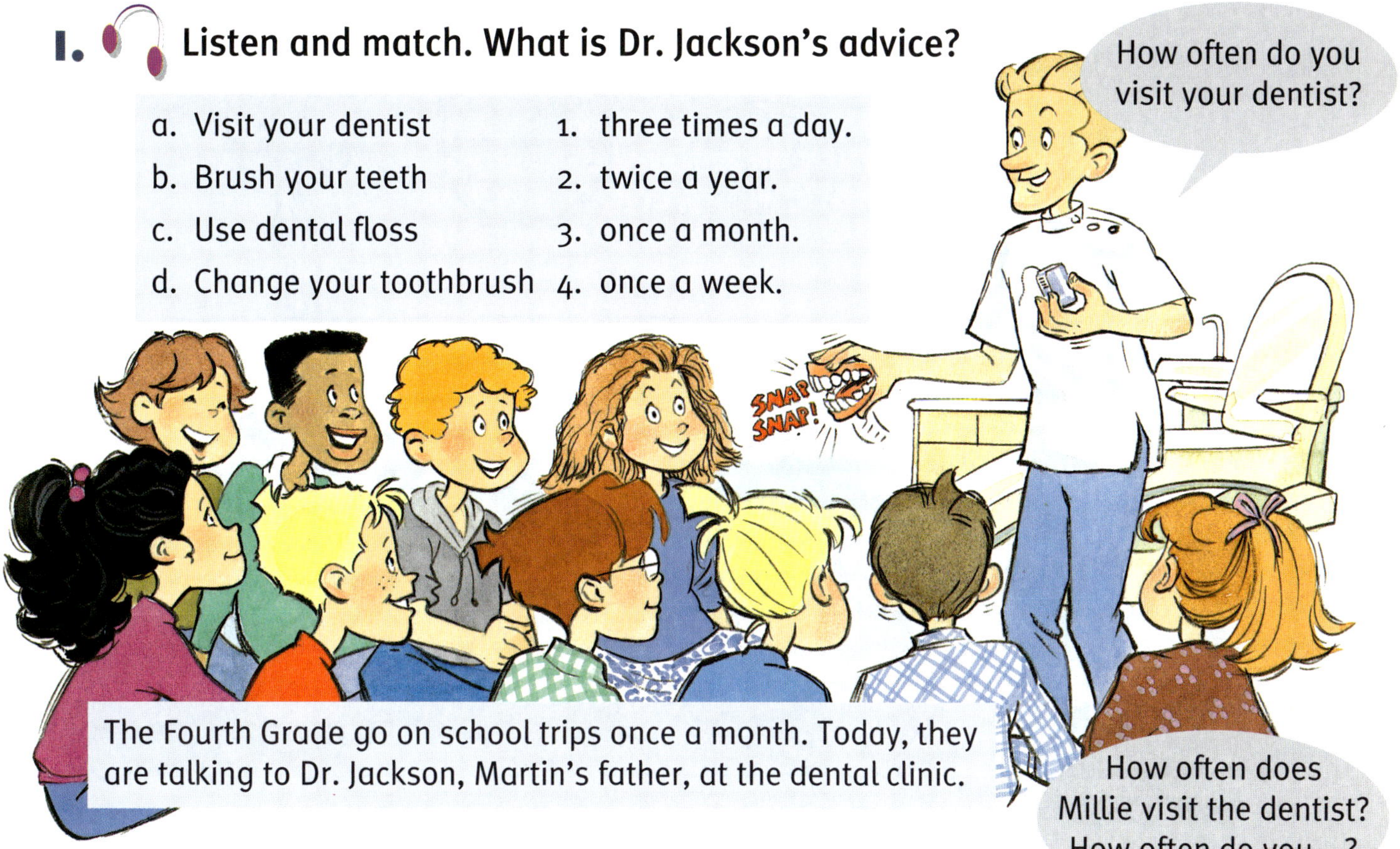

The Fourth Grade go on school trips once a month. Today, they are talking to Dr. Jackson, Martin's father, at the dental clinic.

How often does Millie visit the dentist? How often do you ...?

2. Complete. Ask and answer.

How often do you ...	Boris	Millie	Nina and Ivan	You
visit your dentist?	twice a year	once a year	never	
brush your teeth?	three times a day	twice a day	three times a day	
change your toothbrush?	twice a year	once a year	three times a year	

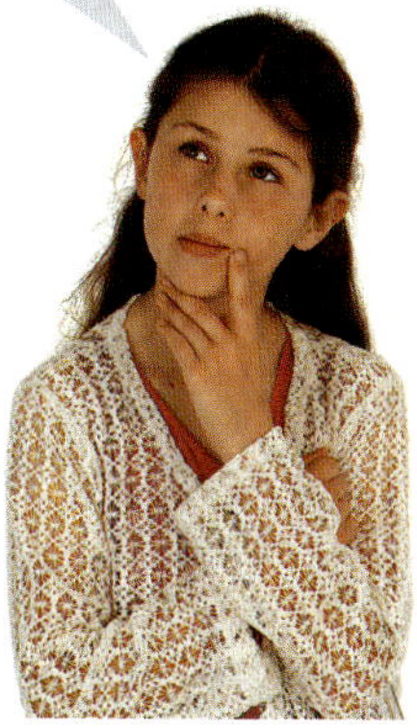

3. Practice. Answer the questions. Write one more question. Ask a friend.

How often do you ...
- make your bed?
- wash the dishes?
- clean your room?
- help do the shopping?
- make your breakfast?

19

It's a quarter to three.   It's a quarter after five.

Lesson 7

 battery

1.  Listen and say.

It's a quarter after eight.

2.  Listen and answer.

Miss Mitzi's classroom clock isn't working.
a. What time did the clock stop yesterday?
b. What time is it now?
c. How much is the battery?

3. Practice. Play the game.

Throw a double!

20

 **Lesson 8**

Detective Tiger

1. 🎧 **Listen and read.**   🎧 detective   footprints   key   ladder   thief

1 Tiger is always the first home. Yesterday he arrived at a quarter after five and he saw footprints in the yard. "Weird!" he said, and he followed them.

2 Then he saw a ladder. It went up to his bedroom window and the light was on! "A thief!" said Tiger.

3 Tiger opened the front door. He took his father's jacket from the peg. He went to his bedroom. There was a person there! Tiger jumped on him!

4 "What are you doing here?" Tiger shouted. "I forgot my key and your window was open!" said Tiger's brother from under the jacket.

2. **Write the words. Write five sentences about the story using each one.**

_____   _____   _____   _____   _____

Lesson 9

Firefighters

1. Read and order.

- [1] There's a fire. Someone calls the emergency services.
- [ ] They jump onto their fire truck and they drive fast to the fire.
- [ ] The alarm rings in the fire station and in seconds the firefighters are ready.
- [ ] First the firefighters rescue the people in danger.
- [ ] The emergency services contact the firefighters.
- [6] Then they put out the fire.

2. Read and do.

Firefighters always wear special fireproof clothes and helmets. They have special equipment. Can you label the special equipment on the fire truck?

ladder   water   hose   oxygen tanks   hatchet

3. For you to do.

a. How often do you have a fire (or earthquake) drill in your school? Describe what you do.
b. Write a list of instructions for the classroom door.

Lesson 10 — Show what you know

1. Write the times.

a. _____

b. _____

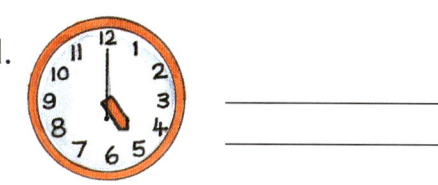

c. _____

d. _____

2. Look at the pictures. Complete the sentences.

a. He _____ (sometimes)

b. She _____ (never)

c. They _____ (always)

3. Complete the questions. Write the answers.

a. How often does Jack have _____ classes?
   _____

b. _____ Penny go _____ ?
   _____

c. _____ Sam and Jean have _____ classes?
   _____

You're a winner!

UNIT 3 In the country

My backpack isn't as heavy as yours.

Lesson 1

n backpack   pair of jeans   penknife
adj expensive   full   heavy   sharp

1. Listen, match and act out.

The children are going camping.

Your backpack isn't as heavy as mine.

2. Compare the children's things.

a. MARTIN / BORIS (sleeping bags)
b. MILLIE / KATIE (boots)
c. BORIS / IVAN (cameras)
d. KATIE / MILLIE (flashlights)
e. MARTIN / IVAN (penknives)
f. BORIS / MARTIN (jeans)

Martin's penknife isn't as sharp as Ivan's.

3. Practice. Play the game.

I have a sandwich.

But your sandwich isn't as big as mine!

24

Horseback riding is more exciting than swimming.

Lesson 2

n fishing   horseback riding   rock climbing   rowing
a difficult   exciting   interesting

1. Listen and act out.

I'd like to go horseback riding. It's more exciting than swimming.

2. Match and talk about the activities.

fishing	dangerous
walking	exciting
rock climbing	difficult
water skiing	expensive
rowing	interesting

Fishing is more interesting than walking.

3. Sing along.

I like the country,
It's more exciting than the town.
You can run up the grassy hills,
And then come rolling down.

I like the country,
It's more attractive than the city.
The trees are more beautiful,
And the flowers are so pretty.

Lesson 3

It's smaller, but it's more comfortable.

n goat   view   **adv** comfortable

1. Listen and answer.

Which is the boys' tent and which is the girls' tent?

2. Look and compare.

a. the sausages
b. the chairs
c. the cameras
d. the sneakers
e. the goats
f. the mountains
g. the tents

3. Complete the postcard.

Dear Mom and Dad:
We are having a lovely time. Our tent is _____ than the boys' tent, but it is _____. And our view is _____ because we can see the river and the mountains. I cooked some sausages for supper. Mine were _____ than Martin's!
See you next Tuesday.
Love, Katy.

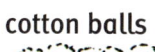

Lesson 4

YOU NEED: red, orange, yellow and black paper, cotton balls, tinfoil, gold stars, scissors, glue

1. Make a campfire picture.

1. Cut the paper into flame shapes.
2. Draw an arch on the black paper. Glue the yellow flames at the top.

3. Glue on the orange flames, and then the red flames at the bottom.
4. Cut out some "logs" from black paper and glue them on.
5. Use pieces of cotton balls for the smoke. Add gold stars and tinfoil for sparks.

2.  Sing along.

Look at the flames,
All orange and bright!
They crackle and spark,
They glow in the night.

Look at the flames,
What a beautiful sight!
They jump and they flicker,
And dance in the night.

Lesson 5 — Check what you know

1. Look, read and circle.

a. The green tent isn't as big as the blue tent.   yes   no
b. The girl isn't as tall as the boy.   yes   no
c. Water skiing is more expensive than rowing.   yes   no
d. The father is more comfortable than the mother.   yes   no
e. The girl is colder than the boy.   yes   no

2. Complete the sentences. Use the words in brackets.

a. Diving is ___more dangerous___ than swimming. (dangerous)
b. Soccer is _____ water polo. (popular)
c. Cooking in the kitchen is _____ cooking on a campfire. (easy)
d. A horse is _____ than a goat. (beautiful)
e. Hotels are _____ than tents. (comfortable)
f. Rock climbing is _____ walking. (exciting)
g. Mountains are _____ than hills. (tall)

Spelling corner

a.    f_____   e. 🎒   b_____
b. 👕   s_____   f. ⛰   m_____
c.    p_____   g. 🐐   g_____
d. 🪵   s_____

28

He took the children rafting.   The river went faster.

Lesson 6

1. Read and match.

a. Then the river went faster and the rocks got bigger – it was much more exciting ... and more dangerous!
b. On Sunday morning, Alex Boski took the children rafting. First, the children put on their life vests and helmets.
c. Then they got into their boats. The river was slow. It was great fun and it was easy!

2. What happened then?

3. Complete Boris's diary.

We had a very exciting day on the river today. Katy ...

There aren't as many apples as before.

Lesson 7

1. Look and answer.

   a. What's for lunch?
   b. What are the children going to do before lunch?

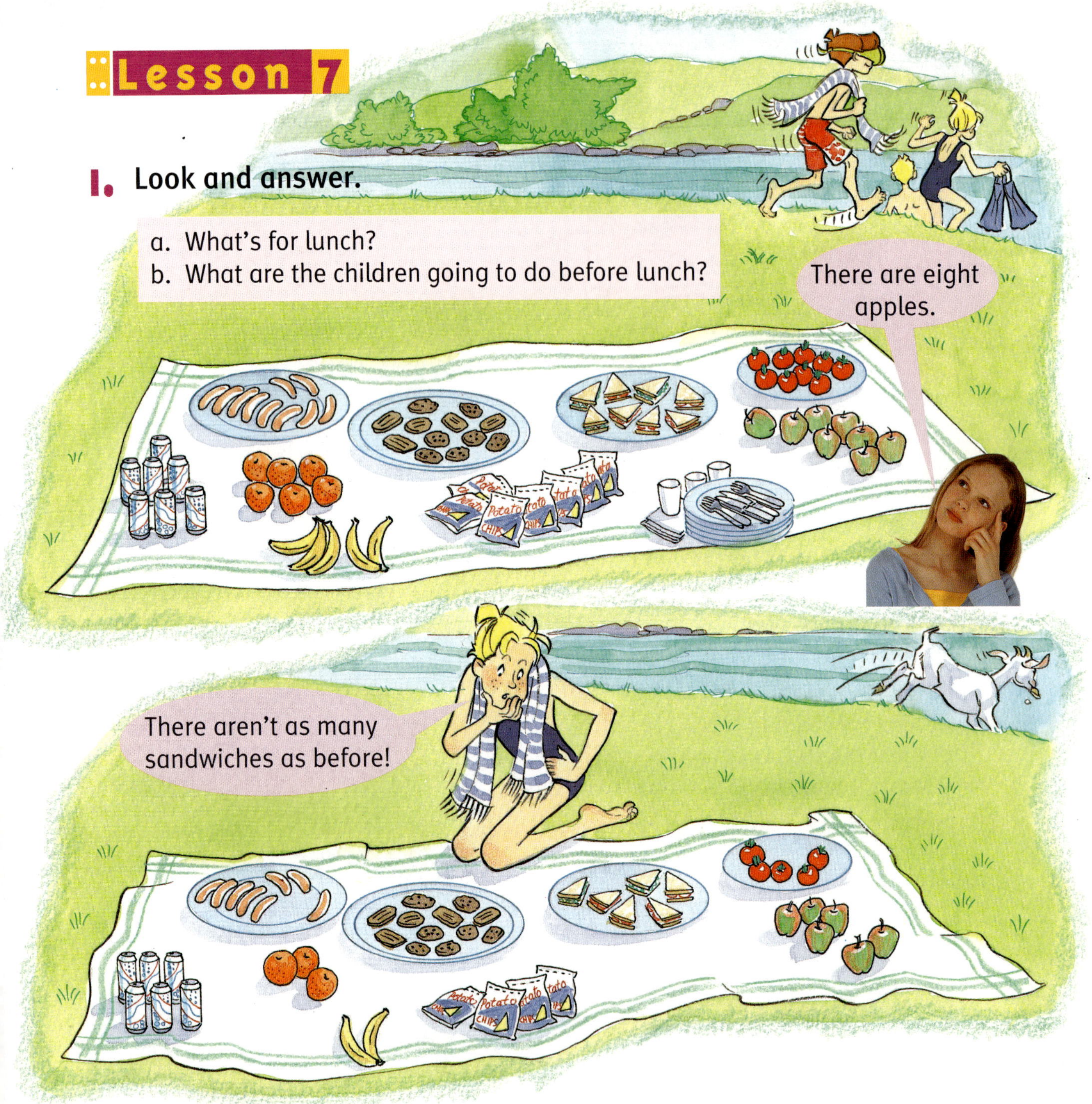

   There are eight apples.

   There aren't as many sandwiches as before!

2. Listen and act out.

   What do you think happened?

3. Practice in pairs.

   Pens!

   I don't have as many pens as you.

Lesson 8 — The black pony

1.  Listen and read.

1 Kit and Bud went to stay with their grandparents for the spring vacation. "Why not go horseback riding tomorrow?" said their grandmother.

2 Grandfather rented two ponies. The black one was bigger than the gray one. "Can I ride the black one?" asked Kit. "No!" said Bud. "I'm older and heavier than you!"

3 "Let's take the narrow road," said Bud. "It's more dangerous than the river road," said Kit. But Bud didn't listen to him.

4 The black pony wasn't as easy to ride as the gray one. "Let's change horses now," said Bud. "No, thanks. I'm more comfortable on this little pony," said Kit.

2. Compare the boys, the ponies and the roads.

Lesson 9

 **Ponies**

1. Listen to the instructor. What are they doing wrong?

a.  b. c.

2. What are the correct instructions?

a. Always wear a riding helmet.
b. _____
c. _____

3. Read and circle the "correct" action.

Going up to a pony
Find out the pony's name. Say the name and go up to the pony's shoulder. Don't shout and don't make any quick movements. You don't want to surprise or frighten the pony. You can stroke the pony's neck or mane.

Giving a treat
When your pony is good, you can give it a treat. Ponies love carrots and apples. Hold the treat with your hand flat and open.

4. Write a list of more working animals.

Ponies are working animals. A working animal is one you can train to help you.

Lesson 10 — Show what you know

1. Complete.

 expensive
 full
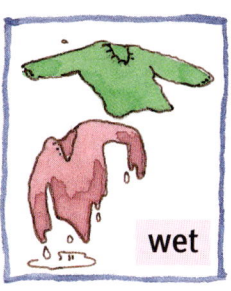 wet
 scared

a. The helmet isn't as _____ the life vest.
b. The red boat _____ as the blue boat.
c. The green sweater _____ as the pink sweater.
d. The children aren't _____ the adults.

2. Complete. Use the words in brackets.

a. Water skiing is _____ than swimming. (expensive)
b. A horse is _____ a goat. (big)
c. A bed is _____ a sleeping bag. (comfortable)
d. Rock climbing is _____ walking. (difficult)
e. A boot is _____ a sandal. (heavy)

3. Spot four differences.

Example: In picture 2, there aren't as many spots on the dog.
a. In picture 2, _____ .
b. In picture 2, _____ .
c. In picture 2, _____ .
d. In picture 2, _____ .

You're a winner!

UNIT 4 The International Center

Lesson 1

I'm from Mexico. I'm Mexican. I speak Spanish.

(n) Japan   Mexico   Egypt   Spain   Canada
(adj) Japanese   Mexican   Egyptian   Spanish   Canadian
Spanish   English   Arabic   Japanese

The children from Fourth Grade are at the International Center.

Where are you from?

1. Listen, complete and act out.

Country: _____
Nationality: _____
Language: _____

2. Act out more.

Where are you from?

34

Lesson 2

1. Read and answer.

Welcome to Japan – your first stop in the International Center. Meet young men and women from Japan. They're wearing traditional Japanese clothes. Visit a typical Japanese house. Try Japanese food at our wonderful Japanese restaurant. And visit our gift shop before you leave!

a. Which is the first place you visit in International Center? _____
b. Who can you meet? _____
c. What can you visit? _____
d. Where can you eat? _____

2. Now write about another "country" at the International Center.

Welcome to ... , your next stop. Meet ...

3. Sing along.

I'm a Canadian Mountie,
My jacket is red.
I wear long boots,
And a hat on my head.

I ride my horse, Maple,
From morning till night,
And honor the law,
And fight for what's right.

They went into the pyramid.

Lesson 3

camel   mummy   pyramid   souvenir

1. Listen and complete the sentences.

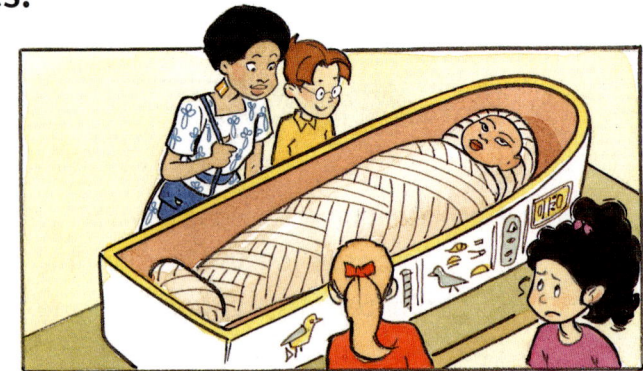

"Egypt next," said Miss Mitzi. She showed the children the "Welcome to _____" sign. Is that what it says?" asked Millie. "Yes. They write _____ script in Egypt," said Miss Mitzi.

The children went into the _____ pyramid. They _____ the model of an Egyptian mummy. "This is _____ _____ than Japan!" said Boris! But Millie _____ _____ it in the pyramid.

2. Read and answer questions. Retell the whole story.

The gift store was like an Egyptian market. Miss Mitzi bought some new earrings there. The children bought some Egyptian cookies and ate them. "They're really good!" said Millie. There was a model of a camel next to the pyramid. The children climbed onto it, and Miss Mitzi took their photograph. "A little souvenir for your parents!" she said.

Place _____ Egypt _____
Who was there? _____
What did they do? _____
What did they see? _____
What did they buy? _____
What did they eat? _____

3. Practice. Tell the class. Write a report.

I went to New York two weeks ago.

What did you do and see?

36

Lesson 4

YOU NEED

paper crayons tape stapler

UNIT 4 — Make It

1. Make a Spanish fan.

1 Put the paper lengthwise and fold it in half.
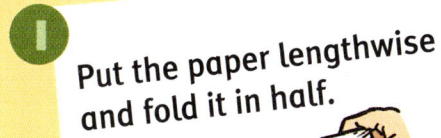

2 Draw flowers in one half

3 Turn the paper and draw flowers in the other half. Do the same on the other side.

4 Fold the paper like this.

5 Fold in the middle.

6 Join the inside sheets at the top with some tape.

7 Staple at the bottom.

8 Open up, and your fan is ready

2. 🎧 Sing along.

We're Spanish.
We come from Spain.
We stamp our feet,
We clap out hands,
And stamp our feet again.

We're Spanish.
We come from Spain.
We shake our fans,
And raise our hands,
And shake our fans again.

37

Lesson 5 — Check what you know

1. Complete the chart.

	Country	Nationality	Language
	Mexico	_____	_____
	_____	Egyptian	_____
	Japan	_____	_____
	Canada	_____	_____

2. Complete the conversation.

Here's a Mexican hat for you. It's a souvenir from Mexico.

    Thank you! When _____?

Two weeks ago.

    Who _____ with?

I went with my family.

    And _____?

We saw pyramids and lovely beaches.

    And what _____?

We ate tacos! They were delicious!

Spelling corner

a.  f_____ d.  r_____

b. p_____

c. e_____ e. c_____

What time is it?

Lesson 6

police officer   the United States

UNIT 4

1. Listen and answer.

   a. Where are they? _____
   b. What time is it? _____
   c. Who isn't there? _____
   d. Where did Boris see them last? _____

2. Look at the pictures. Complete the story.

a. Boris _____ (run)   b. _____ (look)

c. _____ (shout)   d. _____ (talk)

Lesson 7

1. 🎧 **Listen and fill in the form. Act out.**

```
Name: Nina Boski     Age: _____
Description: _____
_____
Wearing: _____
_____
```

2. **Complete the form. Act and write.**

```
Name: Ivan Boski     Age: _____
Description: _____
_____
Wearing: _____
_____
```

3. **Practice.**

What does he look like?

What does she look like?

A lady is looking for you two.

Oh! What does she look like?

I'm thinking of a boy.

He has brown hair and blue eyes.

What does he look like?

Is it Sam?

40

 bottom   escalator   top

Lesson 8

The escalator

UNIT 4 Story Book

1. Listen and read.

1 Amy and her little cousin Graciela were in the shopping mall. Amy wanted to look at some CDs. "Stay here and don't move!" she said.

2 Graciela stood at the top of the escalator. She was very bored, so she rode the escalator down. It was more exciting than waiting at the top.

3 Amy came back. Graciela wasn't there! Amy was worried. She jumped on the escalator and rode down, but Graciela wasn't there.

4 "I lost my cousin! She only speaks Spanish!" said Amy to a police officer. "What does she look like?" he asked. "Well, she has dark, curly hair and …"

Is that her?

2. Answer.

a. What does the police officer look like?
b. What does Amy look like?
c. What language does Graciela speak?

41

 **Ancient Egypt**

1. Listen and circle.

   a. Farmers in Ancient Egypt grew …
      carrots   peas   beans   apples   grapes   cereal
   b. They kept …
      chickens   cows   sheep   goats   horses   ducks
   c. They caught / didn't catch fish.

2. Read. Write a list of facts.

   There were no knives and forks in Ancient Egypt, so people ate with their fingers. There was no sugar, either, but there were lots of bees, so they used honey instead. Fishermen worked in teams. They threw large nets into the water. But fishing in the Nile was sometimes dangerous. There were lots of crocodiles and other wild animals. Women wore lots of jewelry in Ancient Egypt. And they used cosmetics and perfume. And men did, too. And both men and women liked wearing white clothes.

3. Project

   Find out about Egyptian pyramids and Egyptians mummies. Complete this Ancient Egypt Fact File.

Lesson 10 — Show what you know

1. Look at the pictures. Correct the story.

Jay is from Canada. He went to Egypt on his vacation. He ate lots of delicious Egyptian food. He listened to Egyptian music. He doesn't speak Arabic, so he didn't understand the words.

2. Look at the pictures. Write the story.

Mr. and Mrs. Fuji ...

3. Write the question. Draw the person.

What _____ Diana _____?
She is tall and she has long, brown hair. It's curly. She has green eyes.
They're very big and round.

You're a winner!

43

UNIT 5 School projects

She's good at art. He's bad at writing stories.

Lesson 1

🎧 art   geography   math   music

1. 🎧 Listen and complete.

Domino Elementary School Report Card

Name: Nina Boski   Class: Grade 4
Math   7
English   9   Nina's very good at writing stories
History   8
Geography   9
Science
Art
Music   7
Sport   10 especially swimming!

Domino Elementary School Report Card

Name: Ivan Boski   Class: Grade 4
Math   6
English   9
History
Geography   9
Science   7
Art   9
Music   5   Ivan's bad at playing the violin!
Sport   10 especially soccer!

2. Make sentences.

Nina's very good at writing stories. Ivan's bad at math.

3. Practice. Complete the chart. Talk about you.

I'm very good at playing basketball.

subject	excellent	good	not very good	bad
history	✔			
English				
sport				

44

I'm scared of snakes.   I'm not interested in feeding it.

UNIT 5

Lesson 2

adj scared

1. 🎧 Listen and act out.

"I'm scared of snakes!"

2. Complete the questionnaire. Ask three friends.

How many in your class are scared of spiders?

	You	Friend 1	Friend 2	Friend 3
Are you scared of ... ?				
spiders				
the dark				
swimming in the ocean				
going to the dentist				
_____				
_____				
_____				

3. Practice. Write a six-point questionnaire on "What are you interested in?"

Try it out on your friends!

Are you interested in ... ?   yes   no

45

It was too small.

Lesson 3

 fly grass lizard mud rock stones

1. Listen, read and answer.

Boris and Ivan looked for a house for the snake. They found a jar, but it was too small. Then they found a box, but it was too big. Then Boris found an old aquarium. It was perfect!

Did they use …
a. the jar?
b. the box?
c. the aquarium?
Why? Why not?

2. Continue the story.

a. They looked for things to put in the snake's house.
- a rock (big and heavy)
- mud (dirty)
- small stones and grass (perfect!)

b. They looked for a place to put the aquarium.
- yard (cold)
- Boris's bedroom (hot)
- the laboratory (perfect!)

c. They looked for the snake's dinner. They tried to catch …
- lizard (difficult)
- spider (difficult)
- flies (easy!)

3. Complete Boris's diary.

Wednesday
Today I found …

Lesson 4

YOU NEED: an old stocking, newspaper, acrylic paints, yarn

UNIT 5 — Make It

1. Make a snake draft stopper.

1. Stuff the stocking with pieces of old newspaper.

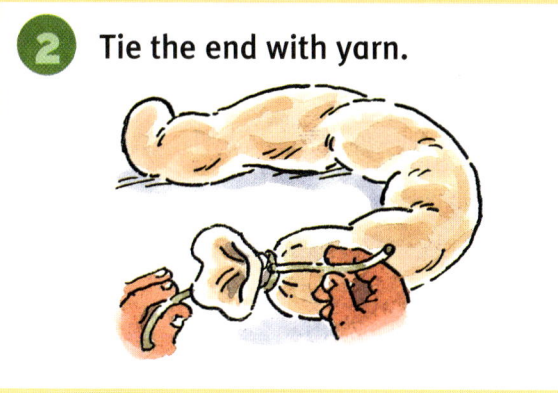

2. Tie the end with yarn.

3. Paint your snake.

4. Put your snake up against your bedroom door.

2.  Sing along.

Jemima is a snake,
Her tongue is very long,
Her eyes are very sleepy,
But her fangs are very strong!
She's good at catching flies,
But she really wants a spider,
To wriggle and squiggle,
And tickle inside her.

Lesson 5 — Check what you know

1. Complete. Use a word from Box 1 with a word from Box 2.

| 1. good   bad   scared   interested | 2. at   in   of   at |

a. She is _____ _____ the mouse!
b. She is _____ _____ swimming.
c. He is _____ _____ the stars.
d. He is _____ _____ making cakes.

2. Answer.

a. Why doesn't she want to go swimming?
Because the water _____ .

b. Why can't he drink the milk?
_____ .

c. Why can't they lift the rock?
_____ .

d. Why can't he catch the lizard?
_____ .

Spelling corner

Write the plurals.

a.  fly   _____
b. 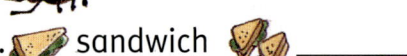 sandwich  _____
c. brush _____

d. cherry _____
e. 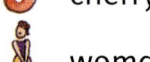 woman 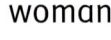 _____
f. child _____
g.  mouse _____

He isn't tall enough.

UNIT 5

Lesson 6

n roof rope skylight   v get through

1. Listen and answer.

a. Why can't Boris get into the lab?
b. Why does he want to?
c. Why does he need Ivan's help to get on the roof?
d. Why can't he get through the skylight?

2. Read and complete.

a. Benjamin, climb onto _____, please.
We're going to help you.
I'm not _____.

b. Can you get through _____?
Now jump down on the table.

c. I can't. It isn't near _____.
Yes, it's _____ enough.

d. Use this _____.

e. It isn't long enough. Help me!

f. Hey!

g. Sorry! We weren't strong _____!

3. Act out your conversation.

It's a beautiful, green snake.

Lesson 7

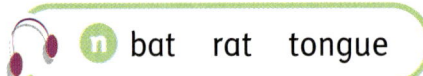 bat   rat   tongue

1. Listen and complete the description. Then act out.

Rasputin is a _____ , _____ snake, with _____ , _____ eyes and a _____ , _____ tongue.

2. Sing along. Then describe the animals.

There are animals in the pet store,
Dogs, cats ... and many more!

There are large, black spiders,
Their tank is near the door.
There are large, black spiders,
In the pet store!

There are little, brown mice,
I think they're very nice.
And there are ugly, white rats,
And funny, black bats.

There are animals in the pet store,
Look at the pictures and talk about more!

3. Practice.

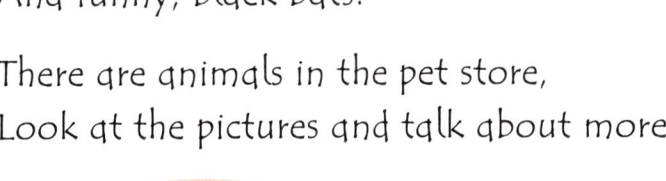

There's a big, red bug.

Describe a pet you know.

I have a little, white mouse with small, pink eyes.

50

Lesson 8 — Herbert's white rat

1. 🎧 Listen and read.

1 Herbert had a new pet. It was a large, white rat. Herbert kept it in a big, yellow cage. It was very good at running. Herbert was very interested in it.

2 Herbert's mother was scared of rats. "I don't want to see it!" she said "It's too horrible!" "It isn't horrible!" said Herbert. "It's a beautiful rat!"

3 Herbert looked after his rat well. One cold evening, he said "Poor rat, you aren't warm enough!" and he went to look for some newspaper for its cage.

4 When Herbert came back, the cage was empty and there was a large, round hole in Herbert's new, red sweater! "Poor rat! Were you hungry?" asked Herbert.

2. What did the rat do after Herbert went for the newspaper? Invent at least five things.

Lesson 9 — Fact File: Spiders

1. Listen and find out.

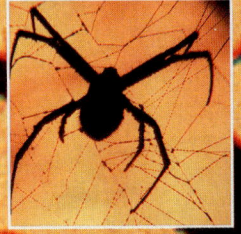

a. Are spiders easy to keep as pets? _____
b. Where can you keep a pet spider? _____
c. What does a pet spider eat? _____
d. How often? _____

2. Read and write the facts.

Let's have a look at a spider. You can see that the spider's body has two parts and it has eight legs. You can't see them, but the spider also has eight eyes.

Web spiders can't see as well as hunting spiders, but this is not important. They don't need to see their food. They can feel the vibrations in their web.

All spiders can spin silk, but not all spiders make webs. Some spiders run around hunting for their food. They don't make webs. They catch flies like a cat catches mice. These hunting spiders have very good eyesight.

Spiders are very good mothers. They lay eggs in a silky bag. Web spiders stay close to the bag. Hunting spiders carry the bag with them, under their body.

a. What does a spider look like?
_____
_____

b. How do spiders find their food?
   1. _____
   2. _____

c. How do spiders look after their eggs?
   1. _____
   2. _____

Lesson 10 Show what you know

1. Complete the sentences with *too* and another word

a rat

a. Its legs are too long. _____
b. Its head is _____ .
c. Its tail is _____ .
d. Its ears _____ .

2. Answer with *enough*.

a. Why can't he drive the car?
   _____

b. Why can't she reach her jacket?
   _____

c. Why can't they lift the piano?
   _____

d. Why can't he catch the lizard?
   _____

3. Unscramble the sentences. Write the story.

a. delicious, popsicle. eating Samantha a is red
b. brown A large, is falling on popsicle! her spider
c. going She's to drop white popsicle the on dress. clean, her

You're a winner!

UNIT 6 Noises in the night

She was running. They were eating.

Lesson 1

🎧 **n** midnight snack   **p** across   **v** bark

1. 🎧 Listen and complete.

a. Katy was running across the _____.
b. Benjamin was sitting under a _____.
c. They were wearing _____.
d. They were having a _____.

2. Continue the story.

"Millie woke up. The moon was shining ..."

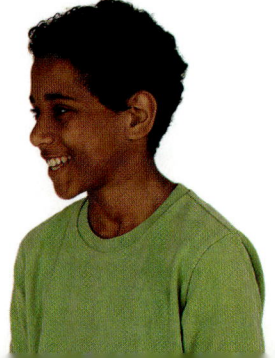
"Boris woke up. The moon was shining ..."

Lesson 2

1. Complete.

Dr. Jackson _____ up. He _____ a lot of noise. He _____ out of the window. All the children _____ under the tree in the yard. They _____ a midnight snack! Frankfurter _____ at Monina. Monina _____ up the tree.

2. Sing along.

The moon was shining,
And the stars were bright.
The owls were hooting,
In the middle of the night.

The stars were twinkling,
For all to see,
But no one was looking,
Except for me!

Lesson 3

He wasn't fighting.

v chase   fight

1. Read and unscramble the words in bold.

It was evening in Domino Street. Suddenly, there was a terrible noise. What was it? Perhaps Boris was doing an **metneripex**. Perhaps Katy and Martin were **ghgiftin**. Perhaps Polly the parrot was **gnsigin**. Perhaps Frankfurter was chasing **nniaMo**. Perhaps the twins were watching a **rororh ovime**.

2. Look and say.

But Boris wasn't doing an experiment. He was working at his computer.

What do you think the horrible noise was?

3. Practice. Play the game.

Someone was playing the drums last night. David?

I wasn't playing the drums! I was reading a book!

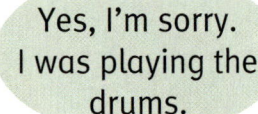

Yes, I'm sorry. I was playing the drums.

Lesson 4

YOU NEED
comb, tissue paper, empty can, shiny paper, yarn, glue, two pencils or pens

1. Make comb tooters and drums.

1 For the tooter, wrap the tissue paper around the comb.
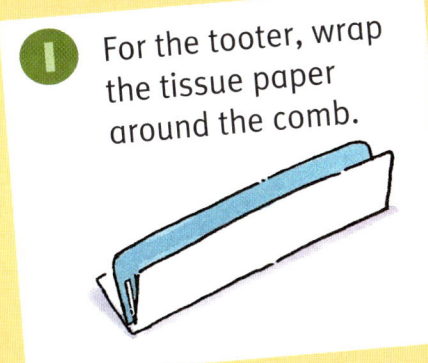

2 For the drum, stick some shiny paper around the can.

3 Stick the yarn around your drum.

4 To play your tooter, put it close to your mouth and "sing" through it.

5 To play your drum, use two pencils or pens.

2.  Sing along.

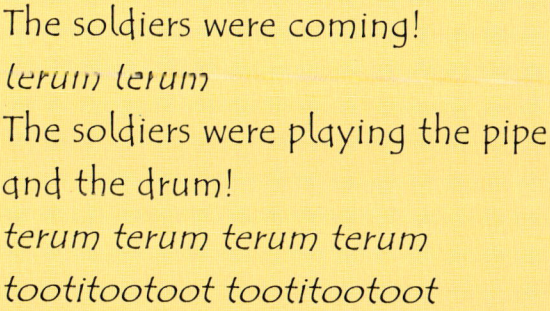

The soldiers were coming!
lerum lerum
The soldiers were playing the pipe and the drum!
terum terum terum terum
tootitootoot tootitootoot

The soldiers were coming!
tootitootoot
The soldiers were coming on horse and on foot!
terum terum terum terum
tootitootoot tootitootoot

57

Lesson 5 — Check what you know

1. Look and complete.

At nine o'clock last night ...

a. The baby <u>was sleeping</u> in his bed.
b. The mother _____ a book.
c. The father _____ television.
d. The children _____ dominoes.

2. Look and complete.

But at a quarter after nine ...

a. The baby <u>wasn't sleeping. He was crying.</u>
b. The mother _____. She _____.
c. The father _____. He _____.
d. The children _____. They _____.

Spelling corner

One consonant or two? Can you guess the rule?

work	→	working	sit	→	_____
put	→	putting	wear	→	_____
shine	→	_____	eat	→	_____
run	→	_____	make	→	_____

What was he doing?   What were they doing?

Lesson 6

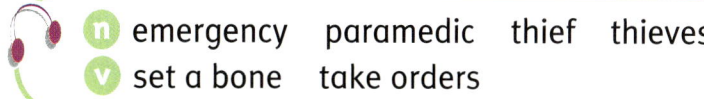

n emergency   paramedic   thief   thieves
v set a bone   take orders

1. Read, listen and number the pictures.

At school, the children were doing a project on the jobs people do at night. The twins had a great idea. They wanted to interview night workers in town. So, last night they went out with their father. First they talked to Harry and Bill …

2. Act out the conversation. Continue.

Miss Mitzi: Who did you find last night?
Ivan: First, we found Harry and Bill.
Miss Mitzi: What were they doing?
Ivan: They were serving tables.
Miss Mitzi: Who did you find next?
Ivan: Next, we found a police officer.

3. Complete the twins' report.

First, we found Harry and Bill. They were
Then …
Next …
Finally …

Lesson 7

1. 🎧 Listen and act out.

2. Ask questions.

Boris's photo isn't very good. What were the owls doing?

a. fly?
b. catch mice?
c. sit on eggs?
d. build a nest?
e. hoot?

3. Unscramble the words and the sentence to find the answer.

kogolni   orf   cime.   eerw   yheT

Lesson 8 — Crash in the night

1. 🎧 Listen and read.

1 Stella and Damien were staying with their grandparents. It was a quarter after nine. "Time for bed!" said their grandmother.

2 It was the middle of the night. Suddenly there was an enormous crash! Stella woke up. Who was walking about downstairs? Was it a thief?

3 Stella found Damien at the top of the stairs. "Were you downstairs?" she asked. "Of course I wasn't. But I heard a noise!" said Damien.

4 The children were scared. A pair of green eyes were coming up the stairs! Damien turned on the light. "Look, it's only the cat!" he said.

2. Write the conversation they had the next morning.

61

Lesson 9  Sound

1.  Listen. Where can you hear these sounds?

   a. ____at the beach____
   b. _____
   c. _____
   d. _____
   e. _____

2. Do some sound experiments.

   a. Find out what sound "feels" like. Hold a balloon ten centimeters away from your mouth. Say something. What do you feel? Now shout something. What do you feel now? What does that show you about sound?

   b. See how sound travels through the air. You need a plastic bottle, a plastic bag, an elastic band, scissors and a candle.

   Cut off the base of the bottle. Then cut a piece from the plastic bag and put it over the end of the bottle.

   Stretch the piece of plastic tight, and use an elastic band round to keep it in place.

   Light the candle. Hold the bottle about two and a half centimeters away from the candle.

   Tap the plastic with your finger tips. What happens to the flame?

   How sound travels
   When you tap the piece of plastic, you make small particles in the air next to it vibrate. These vibrating particles make the particles next to them vibrate, too. The vibrations travel through the bottle and blow out the flame.

Lesson 10 — Show what you know

1. Complete the sentences. Use these words.

read   ride   sing   talk   listen

It was a lovely day yesterday. The family was in the yard. The birds
a. were_____ . Grandma b._____ the newspaper.
Grandpa c._____ to music. The children d._____
their bikes. Dad e._____ on the phone.

2. Write the questions. Answer them.

a. Was Grandpa _____ on the phone? No, _____ .
b. _____ the birds _____? Yes, _____ .
c. _____ Grandma _____ the newspaper? _____ .
d. _____ the children _____ to music? _____ .

3. Read and correct.

a. The doctor was setting a broken bone.
   The doctor wasn't _____ .
   She _____ .

b. The paramedics were answering an emergency call.
   The paramedics _____ .
   They _____ .

c. The police officer was chasing a car thief.
   _____ .
   He _____ .

You're a winner!

UNIT 7 Lunar landscape

It's the newest.

Lesson 1

n documentary   planet   planetarium   solar system
adj far   farthest   large   near

1. Listen and circle.

a. Boris is going to go to the planetarium today.	yes	no
b. At the planetarium you can learn all about the stars and the planets.	yes	no
c. The Redwood Planetarium is very old.	yes	no
d. The Boskis are going to have lunch at home before they go.	yes	no
e. The pizzas at the planetarium are very big.	yes	no
f. Ivan wants to go.	yes	no

2. Read and complete. Talk about Redwood Planetarium.

a. new _the newest_
b. big _____
c. large _____
d. good _____

Redwood Planetarium is the newest planetarium in the United States. It's also the biggest planetarium in the state. It has the largest model of the solar system in the world! Come visit us and see "Our Moon" – the best documentary ever made! Showing every day at 2:30.

3. Look and complete the chart.

The Planets
Biggest: _____
Smallest: _____
Hottest: _Venus_
Coldest: _Pluto_
Nearest to Sun: _____
Farthest from Sun: _____
Closest to Earth: _____

64

Lesson 2

1. Talk about the planets.

Jupiter's the biggest.

2. Sing along.

Mercury, Mars, Jupiter, Uranus,
Neptune, Pluto, Saturn and Venus.
These are the planets going round the Sun,
And don't forget Earth – my favorite one!

Pluto is the farthest – it's ever so far!
Mars is the closest, where the Martians are!
Venus is the hottest – it shines ever so bright,
And Saturn looks good – it has great rings of light.

Lesson 3

n crater   meteorite   surface   telescope
adj clear   deep   high   strong

It's the nearest.

1. Look and listen. Then match.

a. b. c. d.

lightest   strongest
             darkest
deepest
             brightest
easiest to study
highest
             nearest

"Our Moon" – the greatest space documentary ever!

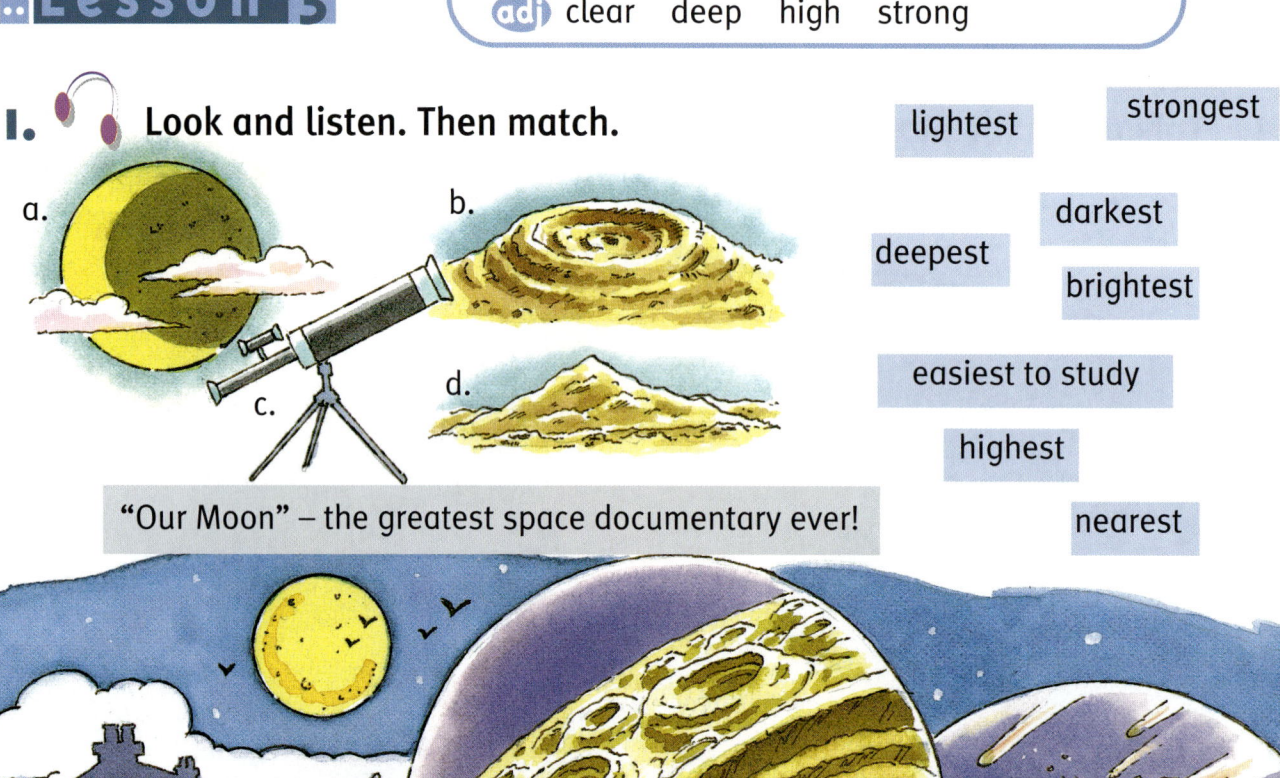

2. Talk about the Moon.

It's the brightest object in the night sky.

3. Practice. Talk about your family.

Who's the oldest?

My grandfather is the oldest. He's 68.

66

Lesson 4

YOU NEED: rocks, tray, tinfoil, plaster of Paris, water, newspaper, spoon

UNIT 7 — Make It

1. Make a lunar landscape.

① Wrap different-sized rocks in tinfoil to make them into "meteorites."

② Cover the tray with tinfoil and put it on the floor with newspaper for protection.

③ Put some plaster of Paris powder into the tray. Pour water onto the powder, mixing it with the spoon.

④ Wait for the plaster of Paris to get thick, but not hard. Then drop your meteorites from chest height into the tray.

⑤ Your meteorites will make craters just like real ones on the surface of the Moon.

2. 🎧 Sing along.

I'm lying in my bed,
Looking out at the light.
The moon is full,
It's the prettiest sight!

I want to be an astronaut,
So I'm going there soon,
To climb the lunar mountains,
And explore the craters of the Moon.

Lesson 5 — Check what you know

1. Read and match.

a. good
b. large
c. hot
d. high
e. old

1. the oldest
2. the highest
3. the largest
4. the best
5. the hottest

2. Complete. Use the words in brackets.

a. Jack has _____ telescope. (good)
b. Jenny has _____ drink. (hot)
c. Jim has _____ hands. (cold)
d. Jenny has _____ hamburger. (big)

Spelling corner

a.  p_____
b. c_____
c. m_____
d.  E_____
e.  s_____
   s_____

It's the most magnificent telescope I ever saw!

UNIT 7

adj amazing   incredible   magnificent

1. Listen and act out.

2. Read and match. Then cover the text and retell the story.

a. They had the most incredible view of the mountains and craters in the Moon.
b. "Can we go in now? I'm cold!" said Millie.
c. It was the most beautiful night. There were lots of stars, and the Moon was full. But it was cold.
d. Boris's mother brought them some hot chocolate. "This is the most delicious hot chocolate in the world!" said Millie.

3. Complete Boris's "thank-you" letter.

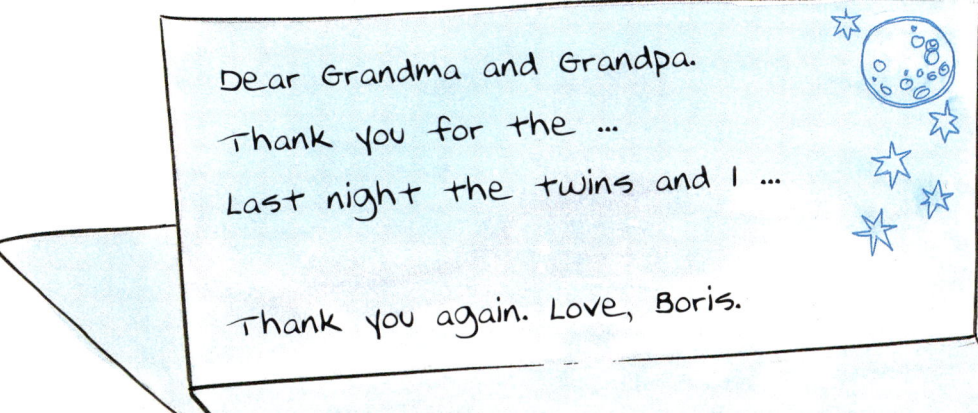

Dear Grandma and Grandpa,
Thank you for the ...
Last night the twins and I ...

Thank you again. Love, Boris.

Lesson 7

🎧 n smile

Who has the biggest balloon/the most comfortable chair?

1. Look and answer.

Benjamin does!

a. Who has the biggest balloon?
b. Who has the shortest skirt?
c. Who has the most enormous sandwich?
d. Who has the most comfortable chair?
e. Who has the longest sweater?

Katy and Martin are having a "Moon party" in their back yard.

2. Continue. Ask and answer.

a. bright shoes?
b. dirty face?
c. large cookie?
d. happy smile?
e. beautiful dress?

3. Practice.

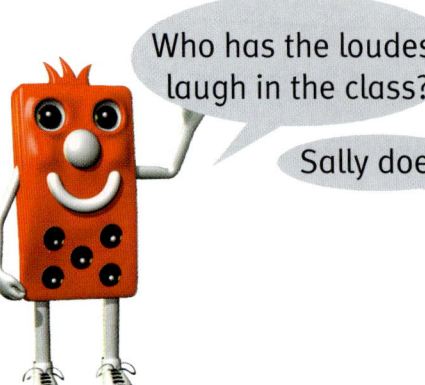

Who has the loudest laugh in the class?

Sally does!

Lesson 8

Surprise on Pluto

1.  Listen and read.

1 There were five spaceships in the squadron, but Commander Clarak was flying the largest and the fastest one, and he landed on Pluto first.

2 Pluto is the smallest and coldest planet in the solar system. And it's the farthest from the Sun. There's no life on it. Well, that's what the scientists say. But ...

3 They were the weirdest creatures, with the most enormous eyes and no legs! They were floating around Commander Clarak's spaceship!

4 The other spaceships landed and the creatures disappeared. "Did you see them?" asked the Commander. "See what?" asked Captain Epwik. "Well, you're not going to believe me, but ..."

2. Write the Commander's report.

> We were visiting Pluto. I arrived first because ...

Lesson 9

Fact File: The Moon

1. Read and complete the Fact File box.

The Moon is our nearest neighbor. It is 384,403 kilometers from us. Getting a man on the Moon was one of the greatest scientific achievements of the last millennium. Neil Armstrong was the first man to walk on the Moon. He stepped onto the surface of the Sea of Tranquillity in July 1969. The Sea of Tranquillity isn't a sea at all (there's no water on the Moon). It's an enormous crater. Astronauts left footprints on the surface. The footprints are still there because there's no wind on the Moon.

Moon Fact File

Distance from the Earth: _____

First man on Moon:

Who? _____

When? _____

Where? _____

What's it like on the Moon? _____
_____

2. For you to do.

a. Find out about the International Space Station, or another space mission. Tell the class.
b. Make a Moon chart
• Divide a large piece of paper into 30 squares (the average number of days in a month).
• Every night look at the Moon. Draw the exact shape you see. Notice how the shape changes in the 30 days. Do you know why this happens?

Lesson 10 — Show what you know

1. Read and name.

_____   _____   _____

Poxi, Tyro and Abu are from a far-away planet. Poxi has the most amazing clothes. Tyro has the longest legs. Abu has the biggest eyes.

2. Complete.

a. deep → _deeper_ → the deepest
b. _____ → bigger → _____
c. sensible → _____ → _____
d. close → _____ → _____
e. interesting → _____ → _____

3. Complete the questions. Use the words in brackets.

a. Who is _____ child in the class? (tall)
b. What's _____ program on TV? (interesting)
c. Which is _____ soccer team in the country? (good)
d. When is _____ day of the year? (long)
e. What's _____ animal in the world? (beautiful)

You're a winner!

UNIT 8 How do you get there?

Go down the street.   Turn left/right.

Lesson 1

 **n** sports center **adv** left right

1. 🎧 Listen and mark the route. Act out.

The Redwood Giants are going to play water polo at the State Sports Center. The twins are going to watch the game.

2. Give directions to Randy Splash.

I'm looking for the Sports Center.

3. Read and find.

The children are going to have pasta with the team after the game. Here are the directions to the Italian restaurant. Mark it on the map.

Leave the Sports Center and turn right, and then turn left. Then go down the street and turn second left. The Italian restaurant is there, right next to the supermarket.

74

1. **Play the game. Go buy ice cream!**

Work in pairs. Choose a location for the ice-cream parlor. Give your partner instructions from the start point. Can your partner find the parlor?

2.  **Sing along.**

I'm looking for the park,
Do you know where it is?
Yes, it's not very far,
You get there like this:

Walk down the street,
And then turn right,
Then walk all the way
To the next stop light.

Then turn left,
And the park is there,
Straight in front of you,
Across the square.

How do you get to the nearest gas station? Turn left at the video store. Go past the drugstore.

Lesson 3

 church   corner   drugstore   gas station   mechanic   video store

1.  Listen and answer.

a. How do they get to the nearest gas station?
b. How do they get to the nearest mechanic?

How do we get to the nearest gas station?

Er ... turn left at the library. Go past the video store, and it's on the corner.

The team is going to play water polo in Pepper Lake Stadium.

2. Ask and answer.

How do we get to the nearest video store?

3. Practice.

From your house, how you get to the nearest store?

Go past the movie theater and turn left at...

76

Lesson 4

YOU NEED: needle pins magnet water paper

UNIT 8 — Make It

1. Make a needle compass.

1 Hold the needle by the eye and stroke it with the magnet. Always stroke the needle in the same direction, from the eye to the point. Use only one end of the magnet.

2 Test your needle magnet on the pins. Does it work?

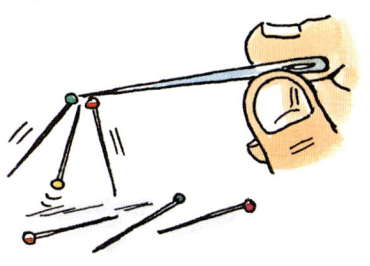

3 Float a piece of paper on the bowl of water. Put your needle on the paper. When the needle stops moving and points in one direction, draw an arrow on a another piece of paper to show the direction.

2. Sing along.

We're lost! We're lost!
What can we do?
　　　Look at a compass –
　　　It can help you!
We don't have a compass,
And it's nearly night!
　　　Well, follow the stars,
　　　They're always right.
It's starting to rain,
We can't see the sky!
　　　So look at a map –
　　　There's no need to cry!
We're here! We're here!
　　　This is the way!
　　　Hooray for the map!
Hooray! Hooray!

Are you north of the equator?
The needle is pointing north.
Are you south of the equator?
The needle is pointing south.

77

Lesson 5 — Check what you know

1. Read the directions. Mark the video store on the map.

Turn right at the church. Then turn left at the end of the park.
Go down the street. The video store's on the corner.

2. Look at the map. Complete.

_____ me, _____ get to the History Museum?

Er … go down the _____ , and turn _____ at the drugstore. Go _____ the movie theater and _____ left. Go past the supermarket. The History Museum is _____ to it.

Thank you.

You're _____ .

Spelling corner

a.
b.
c. s_____

c_____
g ____ s _____
e.

d.
s_____
c_____

d_____
s_____

Give it to me.

Lesson 6

1.  Listen and complete. Use these words.

them him me
her map

Katy: What's this?
Martin: Open it and see.
Katy: I can't!
Martin: Let Millie try. Give it to _____ .
Millie: Yes, give it to _____ , Katy!
         Oh! I can't open it either.
Martin: Let Boris try. Give it to _____ .
Boris: Oh, it's stuck! I can't!
Martin: Let the twins try. Give it to _____ .
Twins: Got it! Look! It's a _____ !

2. Look, read and write.

a. The twins looked at the map. They didn't understand it. They called Boris and gave it to him.

b. _____

c. _____

d. _____

79

Lesson 7

🎧 bridge   cafeteria   route   trophy

It went to ...

1. 🎧 Listen and complete.

The children were _____ a tall pine tree. There was a tall pine tree on the _____ , too! They looked at the route. It started at the _____ . First it went _____ the science lab. Then it went _____ the cafeteria. Then it went to the _____ . Then it turned left and went to the _____ . Then it went across the bridge and stopped at an _____ .

2. Complete the story.

a. The children followed the map. First, they walked to _____ .
b. Then they came to the apple tree and they began to dig _____ .
c. _____ .

Lesson 8

The tennis trophy

1.  Listen and read.

1

Daisy and Ned were doing their homework. "Where's the encyclopedia, Mom?" "It's on the top shelf. Climb up and get it, Ned, but be careful."

2

"Give it to me, Ned," said Daisy. "No," said Ned, "It isn't very heavy." "Give it to her," called Mom from the kitchen. "You're going to break something."

3

Just then, Ned fell. He dropped the encyclopedia. It hit a glass trophy on the bottom shelf. "Are you OK? What was that noise?" shouted the children's mother.

4

"I'm sorry, Mom," said Ned. "It broke." "That was your father's tennis trophy," she said. "He loves it! Well, put the bits in the box and give them to him. Perhaps he can fix it."

2. In pairs, plan the conversation between Ned and his father. Write it. Act it out.

Lesson 9

Fact File: Water Polo

1. Look, read and answer.

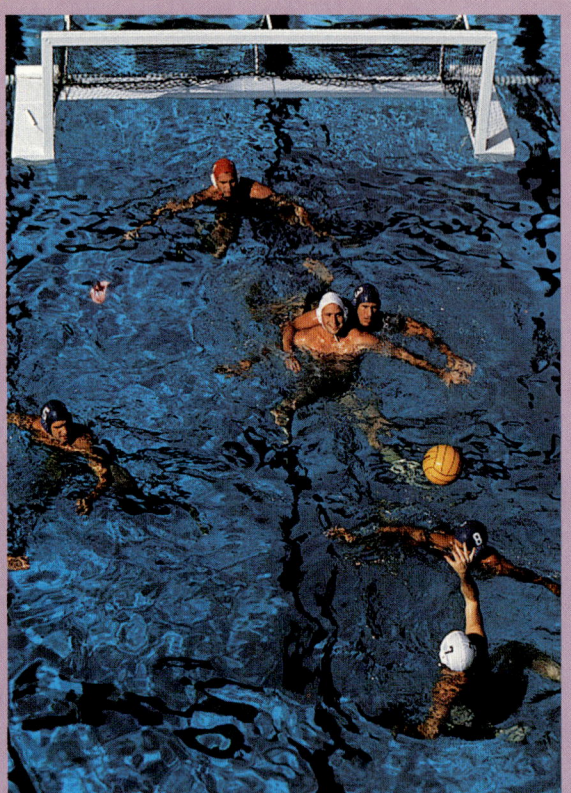

In water polo, there are seven players in each team: six attackers and one goalkeeper. The goalkeepers wear red hats with the number 1, and the other players wear blue or white caps.

A water-polo pool is 30 meters long and 20 meters wide. The water is 1.80 meters deep. There are two goals. They are three meters wide.

You play the game in four periods of seven minutes each. There are two breaks of two minutes and a five-minute break at half time.

Players need to be very good swimmers – and they need to be very strong. You can't stand on the bottom of the pool during the game! The game started in England more than a hundred years ago. Now it's popular all over the world.

a. Which is the goalkeeper in the photo?
b. How long is a water-polo game in total?
c. Mark the dimensions of the pool on the diagram.
d. What can't you do during the game?
e. When and where did game start?

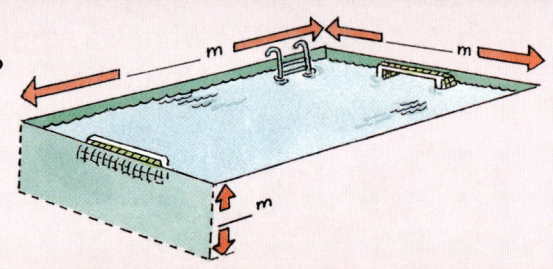

2. Write as many sports as you can under the headings.

Water sports	Other sports
_____	_____
_____	_____
_____	_____
_____	_____
_____	_____
_____	_____
_____	_____

Lesson 10 — Show what you know

1. **Write *him*, *her*, *them* or *me*.**

   a. Susan wants the camera. Give it to _____ .

   b. Give the map to Dad. And give the flashlight to _____ , too.

   c. I can open the bottle. Give it to _____ .

   d. It's their ball. Give it to _____ .

2. **The police officer isn't giving the best directions to the drugstore. Mark the drugstore and the route he gives.**

   The drugstore? Yes. Go down the street and turn left. Go past the church and turn right at the supermarket. Then turn right at the gas station and the drugstore is on the corner, next to the library.

3. **Now write better directions.**

   _____
   _____
   _____
   _____
   _____

You're a winner!

UNIT 9 The girl from Number 5

Lesson 1

She was wearing a skirt.   She was playing basketball.

🎧 n nail

1. **Look and answer.**

   a. Where was Nina?
   b. What was she doing?
   c. What was she wearing?
   d. What was the girl from Number 5 Domino Street doing?
   e. Describe her.

2. 🎧 **Listen and complete. Talk about Kimberly.**

It's her birthday next week.

Name: _____Kimberly Fenton_____
Age: _____
Brother's name: _____
Brother's age: _____
Father's job: _____

84

The bus leaves at nine o'clock.

 member   schedule

UNIT 9

Lesson 2

1. Listen and write the times. Talk about the travel schedule.

Sports Center Notice Board

— Water Polo —

Schedule

8:30   Meet at the university.
_____ Bus leaves.
_____ Stop for lunch.
_____ Arrive at the hotel.

LOST
YELLOW SHORTS

FOUND
BLUE SWIM MASK

2. Talk about their schedule in Miami.

There's a Welcome Party on Monday. It starts ...

Pan-American College Competition, Miami

Welcome Party   Monday 8:30 a.m.
Training session   Tuesday morning 9:00–12:30
Barbecue lunch   Tuesday 1:30 p.m.
First game   Wednesday 11:00 a.m.
Goodbye Dance   Saturday 9:00 p.m.

3. Complete Randy Splash's e-mail to his mom.

To: Mom
From: Randy
Subject: Water polo

Mom: We play in Miami next week. Here's my schedule. The bus _____ at 9:00 on Monday morning. We _____ at the Hotel Beach View in Miami at _____ . We _____ a training session in the morning on Tuesday. Then we _____ our first game on _____ .

Lesson 3

1. What are Brett's questions?

How long do we stay?

When ... ?
Where ... ?
Which day ... ?
What time ... ?
How long ... ?
How many ... ?

Is your Dad in?

No, he isn't

Nina and Ivan
Please tell Brett Fenton:
- the next practice is tomorrow at 10:00.
- we play in Miami next week.
- we leave on Monday.
- we meet at the university at 8:30.
- we stay in Miami for six days.
- we play six games.

2. Act out.

3. Practice. In groups, plan a trip. Find out about other groups. Invite them to join you.

Trip to: _____
Where/When meet? _____
What time/leave? _____
Where lunch? _____
What time/home? _____

We're going to visit the zoo. Come with us!

Great! Where do we meet?

UNIT 9 Make It

Lesson 4

YOU NEED: thick glass, nail polish, masking tape

1. Make a stained-glass window.

1. Put masking tape around the glass so that you don't cut your fingers.

2. Choose a nail polish and paint the outline of the bus. Let the nail polish dry.

3. Choose another color and paint in the windows. Leave to dry.

4. Choose another color and paint in the door and the wheels.

5. Fill in with as many different colors as possible.

6. Stand it near a window so the sun shines through it.

2. Sing along.

We're going on a day trip,
We're going to take a bus.
We're going on a day trip,
A trip for all of us!
The bus leaves at half past eight,
So hurry, children, don't be late!

We're going on a day trip,
We're going to the beach.
We're going on a day trip,
Oh, what a treat!
The bus gets there at half past nine,
And then comes back at supper time.

Lesson 5 Check what you know

1. Complete the sentences. Use these words.

   arrive   have   start   see   leave

   School Museum Trip
   Next Friday
   The bus _____ school at ten o'clock.
   We _____ at the museum at 10:30. We _____ the Ancient Egypt exhibition first. We _____ lunch in the Museum Cafeteria. After lunch, there's a video show.
   It _____ at 2:30.

2. Complete the questions.

   a. What time _____ they _____ ?
      At 10 o'clock.
   b. What time _____ they _____ at the museum?
      At 10:30.
   c. What _____ they _____ first?
      The Ancient Egypt Exhibition.
   d. _____ ?
      After lunch.

Spelling corner

ee or *ea*?

a. water-polo t_____m
b. n_____dle
c. b_____
d. t_____cher
e. p_____s
f. f_____t

How long does it take?

Lesson 6

 airport   commercial   immigration

1.  **Listen and complete the information.**

a. Kimberly's dad flies back from Africa _____ .

b. Kimberly's mother is going to make a _____ tomorrow.

c. Kimberly wants Nina to go with her to the _____ to meet her Dad.

d. They are going to get there by _____ .

e. They need a _____ .

2. Read and find out.

a. When does Flight 309 leave Nairobi? _____

b. When does it arrive at Carter International Airport? _____

c. How long does it take to get through immigration? _____

d. How long does the flight take? _____

e. What time does Captain Fenton get to the main entrance? _____

To	Brett
From	Dad
Subject	Arrival time

Hi, everyone. I'm in Nairobi. Flight 309 leaves Nairobi on Thursday evening. I arrive at Carter International on Friday afternoon at 2:30. It's going to take me an hour to get through immigration. It's a 19-hour flight. Brett, please meet me outside the main airport entrance.
Love to you all, Dad.

3. What's the best bus? Discuss.

Bus departure times from Redwood (Domino Street stop) to Carter International Airport.

Leaves	Arrives
1:30	2:15
2:00	2:45
2:30	3:15
3:15	4:00

The two o'clock bus gets to the airport too early.

Lesson 7

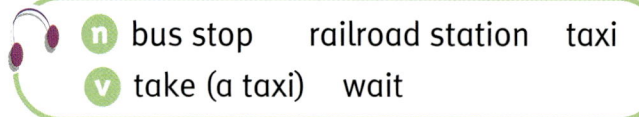

The children were waiting.   The bus arrived.

n bus stop   railroad station   taxi
v take (a taxi)   wait

1. Read and complete the story.

It was Friday afternoon. The children were waiting at the bus stop. The bus arrived. But they didn't know it was the wrong bus!

The children were horrified! They weren't at _____ _____ .

2. Sing along.

The airplane takes off at half past two,
You gotta hurry! You gotta hurry!
So pick up your bags and tickets, too.
You gotta hurry! You gotta hurry!
We're going to call a taxi,

To get us there real fast.
We want to be the first in line,
And not the very last!
We picked up our bags and tickets, too. Don't worry!

Lesson 8 — Fast train, slow train

UNIT 9 Story Book

1. 🎧 Listen and read.

1 Holly and Jake are going to stay with their aunt and uncle by the ocean. They're traveling alone. "Hurry, Jake," says Holly. "The train leaves at a quarter after ten."

2 "Let's buy some candy and magazines for the trip," says Jake. "OK, but don't forget — the train leaves at a quarter after ten. It's ten o'clock now," says Holly.

3 Now Jake is going into the store. Holly is checking the schedule. The fast train leaves at a quarter after ten. And it arrives at Ocean View at twelve o'clock.

4 "What were you doing? Hurry!" says Holly. But they're too late. "The next train leaves at half past ten," says Holly. "But ... it's the slow train! It arrives at six tonight!"

2. Write the children's postcard. Explain their problems.

Dear Mom and Dad,

91

Lesson 9

Fact File: Flying

1. Read and match.

a.

b.

c.

1 One of the earliest flying machines was the balloon. In 1783, two French brothers built the first balloon to carry people into the air – 120 years before the first airplane flew. But balloons were difficult to fly. The first flyers sometimes finished their flight in the most uncomfortable places!

2 Airships were the first machines to fly travelers where they wanted to go. But there was flammable hydrogen in their enormous balloons. So airships were very dangerous. The biggest airship, the Hindenburg, exploded in 1937.

3 The "Flyer" was the first airplane. The Wright brothers made it and flew it in 1903. By 1936, airplanes were carrying passengers at 290 kph! Today's jet planes travel at more than 1,000 kph.

4 The helicopter is the most versatile flying machine. It can go forwards or backwards, straight up or down, or just stay in the air without moving. The Italian artist and scientist Leonardo da Vinci drew a simple helicopter 500 years ago. A French mechanic built the first helicopter that flew in 1907.

2. Find the dates.

a. First balloon flight with people: _____
b. Last flight of the Hindenburg: _____
c. The Wright brothers' first flight: _____
d. First flight by a helicopter: _____

d.

3. For you to do.

Find out about the history of cars or ships. Illustrate your work. Put it up on the classroom wall.

Lesson 10 — Show what you know

1. Read and complete.

Demi Pitt is an actress. Now she's at the _____ . She's going to fly to New York for the première of her movie. The airplane _____ at 10:30 and _____ in New York at 4:00. The movie _____ at 8:00. After the movie, there's a party.

2. Complete the conversation.

Demi: What time _____ our flight _____ ?
Manager: At 10:30.
Demi: And what time _____ ?
Manager: At 4:00.
Demi: And when _____ ?
Manager: At 8:00.
Demi: And what time _____ ?
Manager: At 11:00 – after the première.

3. Write negative sentences.

a. The airplane takes off at six. The _airplane doesn't_ _____
b. The train left late. _____
c. We arrive at the airport at ten.
   _____
d. The flight took a long time.
   _____
   _____

You're a winner!

Everyone is hot.   No one has any money.

UNIT 10 Black and white

Lesson 1

1. Listen and answer.

"Oh! I'm hot!"

"Me too!"

a. What's the weather like?
b. What do the children want to buy?
c. Why can't they buy it?
d. Why don't they want to play basketball?

2. Make sentences.

 "Everyone is hot. No one has any plans."

 a.   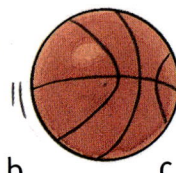 b.    c.    d.

3. Practice. Work in groups of five.

"Answer the questionnaire. Report the results."

Do you have ... ?
- a bike
- a television
- a calculator
- a pet
- a computer
- an uncle in Africa
- a swimming pool

"Everyone in our group has a television. Only one person has an uncle in Africa."

94

No one is interested in anything.

Lesson 2

🎧 costume   theme

1. 🎧 Listen and circle.

a. It's Brett's birthday next week.   yes   no
b. Kimberly's going to have a party.   yes   no
c. It's going to be an Egyptian party.   yes   no

2. Complete the invitation.

Dear friend,
It's my _____ next Saturday, so I'm going to have a _____ .
It's going to be a _____-and-_____ party. Come in a special
_____ , but remember it needs to be _____ and _____ .
The _____ _____ at four and _____ at nine.
(_____ can come in ordinary clothes!)

Address: _____ Domino Street.

3. 🎧 Sing along.

There's a birthday,
Oh, what fun!
Send invitations to everyone!

There's a party,
Please do come,
Everyone's invited to join in the fun!

95

Lesson 3

Everyone is going to come.

🎧 **n** ballet idea ribbon

1. 🎧 Listen and complete.

But Kimberly, I don't have a _____ .

Then make one, Millie. _____ is going to come in a _____ -and- _____ costume! It's a black-and-white party.

Give me an idea! What are *you* going to wear?

I'm going to wear a _____ _____ costume with _____ ribbons on it.

Oh! I know! I can make a white _____ costume with black _____ on it.

2. Act out the other phone conversations.

But, Millie. I don't have a costume!

a.   b.

3. Write one of the conversations.

96

Lesson 4

YOU NEED
black and white paper, black and white yarn, scissors, tape

UNIT 10 — Make It

1. Make black-and-white party twisters.

1 Cut the paper into long strips and fold accordion style.

2 For the tassel, cut five lengths of black yarn 20 cm long and five white ones the same length.

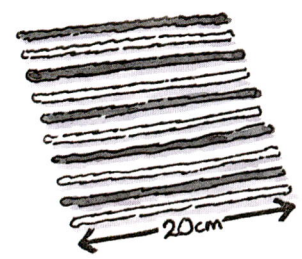

3 Tie them in the middle. Leave a long end.

4 Bend them down and tie them again.

5 Stick your "tassel" on the twister.

6 Braid some yarn to hang your twister from. Hang your twister near an open window and watch it twist!

2. Sing along.

Twist, twist, twist about.
It's party time,
Let's dance and shout!

Twist, twist, twist with me,
It's party time,
As you can see!

97

Lesson 5 — Check what you know

1. Complete with *Everyone* or *No one*.

Let's go home.

a. _____ is wet.
b. _____ is happy.
c. _____ has an umbrella
d. _____ is cold.
e. _____ wants to get home.
f. _____ wants to play in the park.

2. Make mini-conversations by matching the columns.

a. I'm bored.
b. Who loves tests?
c. What's the weather like?
d. Why don't you want to go swimming?
e. Who likes ice cream?

1. Everyone.
2. It's hot.
3. Me, too.
4. No one.
5. It's too cold.

Spelling corner

a.  i_____
b. (butterfly) b_____
c. (snake) r_____
d.  c_____
e. b_____

How about asking your mother?

UNIT 10

Lesson 6

1. Read and complete. Use the words in brackets.

The twins <u>were thinking</u> (think) hard. "What's the matter with you two?" _____ (ask) their father. They _____ (tell) him about the black-and-white party. "But we _____ (not know) what to wear," Nina explained. "Give us an idea." "How about asking your mother?" he said.

The three of them went to look for Mrs. Boski. They _____ (find) her in the kitchen. She _____ (make) cookies. "How about _____ (wear) your black jeans and white sweaters?" she said. "No!" said Nina. "No one is wearing ordinary clothes!"

"Well, I _____ (be) busy now. I can't think! How about _____ (play) a game and then, when the cookies are ready, we can talk about your costumes," said their mother.

The twins _____ (go) into the living room and _____ (get) the box of dominoes off the shelf. Ivan _____ (look) at the dominoes. Suddenly he _____ (have) an idea. "Hey! Nina, How about ... ?"

2. What do you think Ivan's idea was?

Lesson 7

1. Look and answer.

a. What was everyone wearing?
b. What was everyone doing?
c. What were the decorations and the food like?

"Oh, twins! Those are the most wonderful costumes!"

The party was fun. The twins came as dominoes.

Brett was wearing a soccer-ball costume.

2. Read and discuss.

I think Millie's costume was the prettiest.

Whose costume was ... ?
• the funniest
• the prettiest
• the most original
• the best

3. Work in pairs.

Imagine you are going to the black-and-white party.
Decide on a costume and design it. Tell the class about it.

Lesson 8

Ronnie's invention

1. 🎧 Listen and read.

1 Ronnie wanted to be an inventor. "How about inventing a new video game?" suggested Mitch. "Video games are boring. Everyone invents them!" said Magda.

2 Ronnie smiled at his brother and sister. "I'm going to invent something quite different." "Like what?" they asked. "I'm going to invent black-and-white jello!" "Don't be dumb," said Mitch. "No one can invent black-and-white jello."

3 First Ronnie made the white jello. He used jello crystals with no flavor and milk. It was easy. "But how can I make black jello?" he wondered. Then he saw the black pepper pot on the shelf.

4 "Look!" shouted Ronnie. "I did it! How about trying some?" He gave them large bowls of jello. "Ugh!" shouted Magda. "Atishu!" sneezed Mitch. "Don't you like my new invention?" asked Ronnie.

2. Complete Ronnie's experiment notes.

> Today, I invented black-and-white jello, but no one liked it. First I ...

101

Lesson 9

Fact File
Dominoes

1. Read and answer.

a. Who played dominoes first?
b. What's the difference between the three types of dominoes?
c. Which player starts the game?
d. Which player wins the game?

Dominoes is a very old game – one of the oldest games in the world. The Chinese played dominoes first in the twelfth century, but their dominoes were very different from ours. Chinese dominoes had dots on the front and on the back. Ours only have dots on one side. Another domino game developed in Alaska. There, the Inuits played with a 148 domino pieces. We play with only 28 dominoes.

The usual set of dominoes is marked in the following way. Complete the sequence.

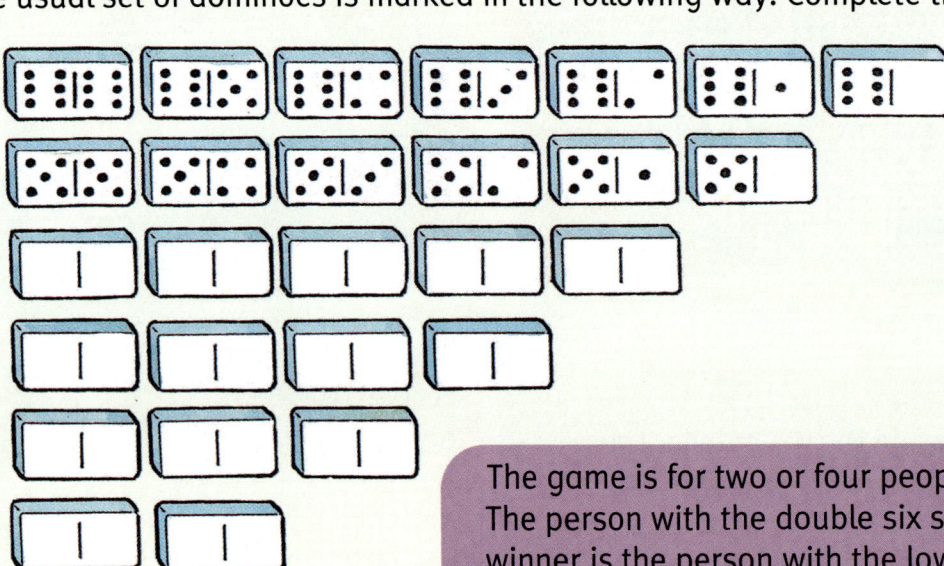

The game is for two or four people. The person with the double six starts. The winner is the person with the lowest number of points (or dots) at the end of the game.

2. Answer the questions.

a. Can you play dominoes?
b. What other board game can you play?
c. Which is your favorite board game?
d. Some of the newest games are video games. Which video game do you like and why? Write five sentences.

Lesson 10 — Show what you know

1. Complete. Use the words in brackets.

It was a lovely day for a barbecue. The sun <u>was shining</u> (shine). Dad _____ (make) hamburgers. Mom _____ (cook) sausages. Grandma and Grandpa _____ (wait) for lunch. "How can I help?" asked Sandy. "How about _____ (serve) the sodas?" said her mother. "And how can I help?" asked Danny. "How about _____ (get) the jello?" Mom said to Danny. So Sandy _____ (serve) the sodas and Danny _____ (go) into the kitchen for the jello.

Danny _____ (come) into the yard with a very large fruit jello. "That's the _____ (big) jello I ever saw!" said Grandma. Just then, Tubby the dog _____ (jump) up and the jello _____ (go) flying through the air. It _____ (fall) on Grandpa. "Yes – and it's the _____ (delicious) jello I ever had," said Grandpa.

2. Complete with *everyone* or *no one*.

a. In picture 1, _____ is in the yard.
   _____ is eating.

b. In picture 5, _____ is mad.
   _____ is laughing.

You're a winner!

103

GAME 3 — Five in a Row

yesterday	scared of	sometimes	want to be	not as ___ as ___
good at	too	How often ...?	interested in	now
faster	last month	never	enough	bad at
best	always	easier	more difficult	last week
every day	too	more expensive	How often ...?	enough

Spelling Wheel

GAME 8

111

Macmillan Heinemann English Language Teaching,
Between Towns Road, Oxford OX4 3PP, UK
A division of Macmillan Publishers Limited
Companies and representatives throughout the world.

ISBN 0333 92556 4

Text © Angela Llanas and Libby Williams, 2001
Design and illustration © Macmillan Publishers Limited, 2001

Heinemann is a registered trademark of Reed Educational and Professional Publishers Limited

First published 2001

All rights reserved; no part of this publication may be
reproduced, stored in a retrieval system, transmitted in any form, or by
any means, electronic, mechanical, photocopying, recording or otherwise,
without the prior written permission of the publishers.

Design by Sue Vaudin
Illustrated by Maureen Gray, Lynda Knott, John Peacock, David Till, Dave Williams
Cover design by Mark Duffin

The authors and the publishers would like to thank the following for permission to
reproduce their photographs:
Bruce Coleman p 9 (tr); Corbis pp 10 (br), 19 (t), 52 (tm), 62 (br); Eye Ubiquitous pp
9(tl),10 (br, bm), 47, 75; Haddon Davies © MHELT; pp 4, 5, 10 (mr, ml), 15(b), 16, 19(b),
24, 26, 30, 34, 35, 36, 44, 46, 49, 50, 54, 55, 56, 59, 62 (bm), 64, 65, 69, 72, 74, 76, 79,
80, 85, 86, 100; Image Bank pp 17, 25, 32 (mr); Life File p 15(t); Stone pp 52 (tr, tl), 67;
Telegraph Colour Library; pp 32 (tr)

The publishers wish to thank Nethan Burke, Jessica Mole, Ben Robinson and
Hannah Roe.

Printed in Colombia by
Quebecor Impreandes, S.A.

2005 2004 2003 2002 2001
10 9 8 7 6 5 4 3 2 1